Mommies Working Together

http://www.PC-Mommy.com

PC-
Mommy

123 Ways to Run Your Family With Microsoft
Office® and Get A Promotion

Qwin J. Humphries, M.Ed

PC-Mommy;
Run Your Family With Microsoft Office® and Get A Promotion
Qwin Humphries, M.Ed.

Visit the PC-Mommy Online Learning Community for learning and teaching opportunities.
http://www.PC-Mommy.com

Library of Congress Control Number: 2007943343

ISBN: 978-0-6151-7382-5

CONTENTS

Acknowledgement

This book is dedicated to my wonderful team: my family. You all cannot say it has been boring. John, Ashley, and John John; you all have been a great inspiration for me to think outside of the box and I love you all so very much. I never knew being a corporate career woman and the mother I wanted to be was going to lead to me to such conflict that I would change the game. However, it did and what a magnificent result of sheer innovation. Thanks for hanging in there and being my experiment. I hope you all have a jagged computer edge when you grow up and enter the workforce. Thanks to my mom and dad, Jean and Jerry Coleman, for helping me by hassling me to do computer tasks for them like so many parents do. In the end they learned to use the computer for themselves (I am so proud of my two students). I give special thanks to my brother, Jerry Coleman III who has been a great support for family in many ways. He is always there when I need him from babysitting to helping with my endeavors. Though I still consider myself the resident computer expert of the family, everyone else is also tech savvy now.

I also thank Dr. Rosalind P. Hale who gave me my first chance to do what I love, teaching, after a significant career change. A special thanks to Tanji Lee for the feedback on my book. I would like to offer a huge appreciation to Juanita "Nita" McGlond for helping me with the edits of the book. You were a great help. Most of all, thanks to God who is a mastermind in deed. When I clearly could not see the way even when I thought 100% I knew where I was going, I stepped out with my faith and God delivered me through closed doors and over invisible floors. God does have a plan and we have a destiny.

Introduction

Carol Brady had Alice; I have a computer with Microsoft Office®. Hum . . . Maid . . . vs . . . Computer?

- **I do not have to pay money . . .**
  – It's ALREADY on my computer.
- **I can enhance what I know; my technology skills . . .**
  – I am familiar with the software from work.
- **What I use at home . . .**
  – I can take it back to the job and advance my career.
- **I can save time . . .**
  – I have the program at work and can work on these things at the job.
- **I can help my children . . .**
  – They will become self sufficient and technology advanced.
- **I can help myself . . .**
  – When my family communicates we all are happy.
- **The things in this book can be a collaborative family effort that we all can show off together.**

Although this book is not the confessions of a non-domestic mother, I confess; if my family wants collard greens and pinto beans I will check www.google.com for the nearest soul food restaurant and print the menu so we can call ahead. Even a recipe posted to the web will not help a mom like me. Lord knows I have tried to be June Cleaver, but simply helping my kids with homework showed me I could not, would not, shouldn't even home school them. It is not my level of education, but my sanity. Yet, I am a superstar when it comes to work so the least I could do is make enough money to buy a nice house, send them to a great school, hire a tutor, and afford the good eats. I just did not realize the motherly sacrifice involved until I missed out on all of the good stuff while at work. I want to be a room mom too . . . on second thought maybe a consultant to the room mom.

So I eventually realized I was never going to be the traditional mom, but I still have lots to offer. That is when the idea "use your computer to organize your home" popped into my brain. The very computer skills that landed me so many promotions at work really could help me get my family operating more smoothly. After all I was so much more organized at work than I ever was at home. So I came up with some rather simple yet effective "technology" solutions for a busy mom to use with her kids, husband, and

www.PC-Mommy.com

self. I am not just talking about career moms because stay-at-home moms are really busy as well. Dads can do them too.

Instead of me calling out my son's spelling words, he calls them out to himself in a narrated slideshow. He is so tickled listening to his own voice. Best of all, he came to me a year later about a similar idea he approached with his friends using the narrated skills I taught him. Whose mom does that, huh room mothers?

My daughter checks her math homework in Excel on her own. Set it up one time; use anytime. She loves it! I love it!

Is it not cool for a 4th grader to pass out self made business cards even though they are printed on regular flimsy typing paper? Who needs card stock at 9 years old? My daughter was so cool that she started a little side business making cards for her friends before the school shut her down and I realized she was using all of my ink.

In regards to communication, we improved the family system by implementing the email, task manager, and a family/business contact lists. Now I simply send my kids a chore task via email. They have to accept and I receive the acceptance in a reply message. Once completed, they simply click completed on the status menu and I receive an email confirmation. On the other hand, I have so much on my mind while balancing all my roles as a woman that I have my kids to create requests for me when they need special supplies or field trip money for school that I simply add to my calendar. That way I do not forget to complete the tasks.

So here you are busy mothers. This book is my gift to show you some alternatives that will not only help you balance work against family management, but also help you to help your kids become self sufficient while you get ahead in a technology dependent world. You may even advance your career as I did. These fun tips are efficient and the long term effects are very desirable. If you use these programs for task management at work, you can better use them at home for your family. Once they learn how to perform these computer skills, they will be so "self" engaged you will be left with more time to be the mother you want to be rather than stressed out and tired of being tired. I found that they helped me and my family in invaluable ways never thought imaginable. They do not work miracles though. [Click], [click]!

LEGEND

•	**BLUE BOLD**	Menu Item
•	GREEN BRACKETS	Click your mouse
•	**<u>BOLD UNDERLINE</u>**	Select an item

How to select text?

Click the mouse at the beginning of the text to be selected. Hold and drag the mouse until the text contains a shaded/highlighted background to indicate it is selected.

How to select an image?

Click the image with your mouse.

When do I left click?

The word "click" by default means to left click. Simply press the left button of your mouse. "Right click" indicates to click the right button of the mouse and will always be referenced as "right click".

More details can be found at www.PC-Mommy.com Online Learning Community.

1 All of this is the computer?

Technically no; practically yes. The first thing you need to do is set your computer up properly *(feel free to skip this chapter if your computer is already setup)*, but you need to know what is what and where it goes. To spare you the boredom, a computer is basically a combination of <u>in</u>put and <u>out</u>put devices. In other words we have things to allow "us" to communicate with the computer (input) and things for "it" to communicate back to us (output). Let us take a look at these items and make sure you have the required components:

1.1 Computer Components

1.1.1 Hardware

Hardware is the physical part of the computer.

Table 1.1

Part	Type	Plug Here (small images may be etched on the case)	Usage
Monitor	It puts out to you		Viewing screen
Speakers	It puts out to you		Produces sounds

Part	Type	Plug Here (small images may be etched on the case)	Usage
Printer	It puts out to you	Parallel or USB connected	Paper documentation
Headphone and Microphone	It puts out to you You put into computer		Sounds
Tower	Processing	(power button symbol for computer related devices)	The brain that processes the information
Mouse (scroll control)			Rolling clicker to navigate around

Part	Type	Plug Here (small images may be etched on the case)	Usage
Keyboard	You put into computer		Input Information
Storage devices – Floppy, CD, Jump Drive	You put into computer and your computer puts out to you	Jump Drive – USB	Retrieve and save information
Ethernet Internet / Router	You put the Internet or Network into your computer		Plug one end into DSL/Cable router and the other to your computer
Image devices - Scanner, Digital Camera	You put into	Most usually have USB connections as shown with the Storage devices.	Retrieve images. Plug when in use, unplug when not in use

3

Connectors: The usage varies by device - Just as appliances have different ends such as 2 prone and 3 prone plugs; computer devices have different ends. Never force a connection. If you line them up properly they should just glide in. Otherwise you may be trying to insert a connector into the wrong plug. Some common ones include parallel, serial, and USB.

Just a note: your computer may have color coordination and/or images next to the connection to ease the setup process. Separate your wires and take one step at a time. Do not panic.

1.1.2 Software

While hardware is the puppet you see, software is the puppet master running the show. Software is the program that processes on the computer to allow you to accomplish a specific task depending on that particular software design. In this book I focus on one specific group of software because it is usually bundled and already

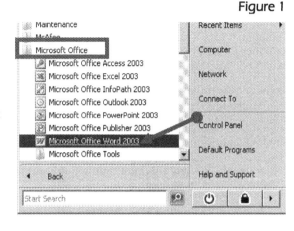

Figure 1

available on your computer. This is of course Microsoft Office®. I have this particular set of software on my computer and I am all about saving money by using what I have. So if your computer has Microsoft Office® you are set to go. If not; do not worry. You may simply apply the ideas using similar software. Hey – I am not getting paid by any software vendor. I also use a free screen shot application called Screen Hunter 4.0 to capture the figures you see throughout my book.

Figure 2

To see *your* different software:
- [Click] your **Start** button located at the bottom left corner of your screen.
- Then [click] **All Programs**. (The arrow means there is more to follow if you move in the pointed direction)
- Next, slowly move your mouse to the right.
- Then move up/down to **Microsoft Office** and [click] your mouse on the arrow.
- Move right again and there is the list of all of your office software as shown in Figure 1.
- [Click] on the one you would like to open. In this case we will [click] on **Microsoft Word**.

2 How do I get around computer land?

Your kids may be more up to speed than you think. In the event they are not familiar with navigating the computer you will have to introduce them to the basic skills. My ideas and activities allow you to work together as a family. If "you" cannot get around though, be sure to introduce yourself to the computer first.

2.1 The Main Screen

Figure 3

Figure 3 reflects what we typically see when the computer is powered on with the exception of the picture of my kids of course.

Think of your computer as your desk where you store your job files and other paperwork. Now when you take a seat at your desk the first thing you will notice is what's on top of your desk. Is it messy or organized? Nevertheless, this image represents your "**desktop**". Trust me; it can get as cluttered as a real one. The picture of the kids in the sand is my "**background**". The little images to the left of the screen are called "**icons**" or shortcuts to take us places within the computer with a simply double click. Keep the things you use most on your desktop as you would a stapler and tape dispenser on your desk.

2.2 The Main Menu

These are your basic command menus that you will see within most of the applications discussed in this book. Sometimes you may see a few more or less depending on the intended purpose of the application. For instance Microsoft Word® has a Table menu while Microsoft Excel® does not. However, these basic commands can be compared to how we handle a hard copy manila folder in a file cabinet. I will elaborate.

Figure 4

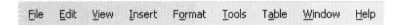

File   Edit   View   Insert   Format   Tools   Table   Window   Help

File – The manila folder *(maintain your files)*. For example, you can choose to put away your document for later retrieval by saving it. Simply [click] on the **File** menu and then [click] **Save**. You can also choose to **Print** all or part of your document using the Print option or simply **Close** your file to put it away.

Edit – Revisions *(update, delete, find things in the manila folder)*. You can edit your document in many ways. You may also perform tasks such as undoing or redoing your last couple of revisions.

View – Visualize and lay out your file *(the way you see your documents in the manila folder on the screen)*. See your document in different layouts such as how it will look printed (Print layout), reading in a two page book style (Reading layout), or rulers to know the precise location on the page.

Insert – Add or insert items into your document. You would use these options to add page numbers, a picture, a link to a file or webpage, etc.

Format – Look and style of your document. Use these options to change the look of the characters you type into your document (*Fonts*) and also the overall appearance of document.

Tools – Some useful resources to help you along the way such as a Dictionary, Thesaurus, Letter/Label creators, etc.

Table – Allows you to add a neat table at any point in your document to organize information. The hardware components in this book are listed in Table 1.1.

Window – Toggle between opened files.

2.3 Tabs

Just like a manila folder has a tab where we write names to help us easily file and sort them into file drawers, computer applications often have options that let us sort through the tabs to navigate to the places we need to go.

Figure 5

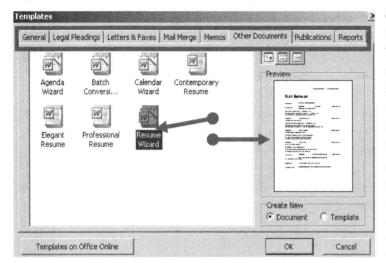

In the case of Figure 5, Templates is the file drawer, and General, Legal Pleadings, etc. are the tabs we sort through to get what we need. When you click a tab, you will see all of the related options for that particular tab.

A preview pane (think of a window pane) is located on the right side of this Templates folder. You use it to take a peek at a template in the Templates folder. A template is just a pre-designed document that is useful when you want to be consistent and do not want to create a document from scratch. To preview a contemporary resume template for example versus an elegant resume template just click on each template one at a time.

3 Microsoft Who?

3.1 Why Is This Book About Using Microsoft Office 2003?

It is on my home and work computers. For the last few years or so, I believe Microsoft has included some of their most widely used software with our computer purchases. Additionally, many of us are already familiar with the basics of the software and their applications or usages because our work computers have similar versions that we use to create letters, reports, enter customer information and so forth. Would not you rather take on something you already had some idea about? I do not want to spend the money on the new version just yet especially while the old one still does the trick. So let us save money and use what we have. We are mothers after all. If you have other programs such as Word Perfect® or Microsoft Works® just follow my ideas, but implement them with your corresponding application. You should be able to implement the concept of my ideas even in the new 2007 version.

3.2 What's the Microsoft skinny?

For the purpose of this book we will focus on the most commonly used and included applications in the software bundle. Just to give you an idea of the function of each application I will break them down. A common element of each is the important command menu just previously discussed (File, Edit, etc). You really need to think in terms of logic when it comes to the menu. For instance, if you would like a picture on your cover page then you have to think of it as though you are attempting to "Insert" something on your paper. So you would open your **Insert** menu. If you want to make your name large and red, you need to think about it as though you are changing the look of your document. In that case you would open your **Format** menu. Get the drift???

3.2.1 Microsoft Word®

THE WORD PROCESSING APPLICATION. It is primarily applied (hence application) in creating documents. Think of it as basically typing on a page like an old fashion typewriter without the need of liquid paper for correcting. *However, word processing can be used for a number of useful things in the home front for other than merely typing a paper. Get ready to change your life for good.*

3.2.2 Microsoft Excel®

THE SPREADSHEET APPLICATION. It primarily serves as a ledger of rows and columns. If you can remember the old thick ledger books for accounting or even better your checkbook then you can visualize a spreadsheet used to track tons of numbers using rows and columns. *Yet, spreadsheets have the ability to compute powerful calculations, sort information, and manipulate data faster and more accurately than a human. Do not worry; we are too innovative to be stuck within lines.*

3.2.3 Microsoft PowerPoint®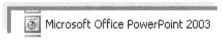

THE PRESENTATION APPLICATION. The primary purpose is of course to create Slide Shows. Unlike the projectors of the good old days or even the transparencies and school overheads, this application enables you to combine colorful designs, graphics, information, and links that take you to any place a computer can visit.

3.2.4 Microsoft Outlook®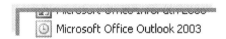

THE TELECOMMUNICATIONS APPLICATION. It is used primarily for email purposes. Still, this application can connect to many web based emails such as Hotmail, Yahoo, etc. Then it offers exceptional task and contact management options to help track your time, schedule meetings, maintain address books, and so much more.

4 What's the Word?

Remember that this application is most like the typewriter (but with many more capabilities). On the job we type reports for our companies. However, at home we can expand our horizons. The main menu commands are **File, Edit, View, Insert, Format, Tools, Table, Window,** and **Help**. Currently my daughter has a printer in her room that is shared on a network which gives my son access to it as well. Prior to this setup, I would have them attach the items they wanted to print to an email and send it to me to execute the printing. That worked out well and they got quite a bit of practice with attaching files to an email – something I find a few of my adult students have not mastered quite yet. You may want to try this method with your family and eventually create a home network.

Here is how to implement word processing for your family.

4.1 Postings

4.1.1 Rules Of The House

Figure 6

We know the main excuse for breaking the rules of house is "I did not know that was a rule". Not only can you nip that in the bud, you can get your family to help you. Why type a list when you can setup a family activity with the kids? They should type the list so they clearly know the rules. Then they cannot argue they do not know them if they were the ones to create the document.

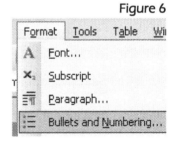

- Start them off in a blank document by opening Microsoft Word®. If you do not see a shortcut on the desktop, just [click] the *Start* button in the bottom left corner of your screen, then **choose** *All Programs,* then **choose** *Microsoft Office,* then **choose** *Microsoft Word® or the word processing program you have on your computer.*
- Then have the kids add a title such as "The Humphries House Rules by Ash" *(let them take the credit because Grandma will see them posted when she comes to visit).*

- Since we want the style (hence look) to be a numbered list or bulleted list, **select** "Bullets and Numbering" from the **Format** menu as shown in Figure 6.
- [Click] on the **Bulleted** tab and **select** a bullet style of your choice.
- If you prefer numbers then [click] on the **Numbered** tab and **select** a style you like best.
- [Click] the Customize button if you do not see a style you would like to use. See Figure 7 for an example.
- If you selected to customize your list then you will need to make some choices as shown in Figure 8. Press ok when done.
- When you or your child type the first item and press the enter key, the next item will automatically insert with a new bullet or the next number in sequence. Even if you get down to number 5 and you

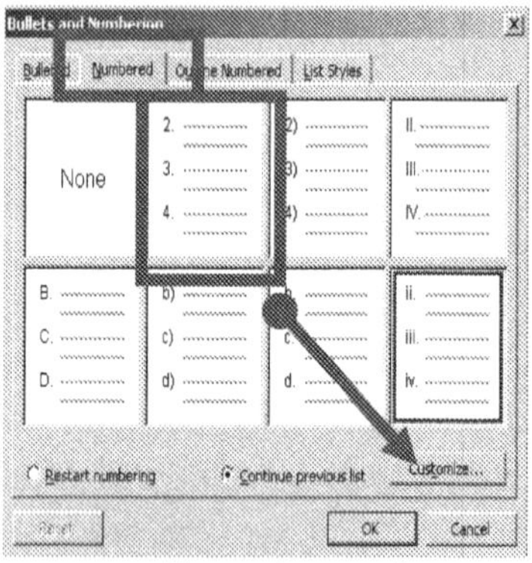

Figure 7

realize you missed one between 3 and 4 you can just press enter when you get to the end of the last word of bullet number 3. A new blank number 4 will insert and your previous number 4 will become 5 automatically.

- Do not forget to save your document.
- Just [click] **File** on the menu.
- Then [click] **Save**.

Once the household rules are posted up on the wall your family will be so proud of the job they did that maybe they will remind their friends to follow your household rules. Just brag about the great job they did in creating them.

Figure 8

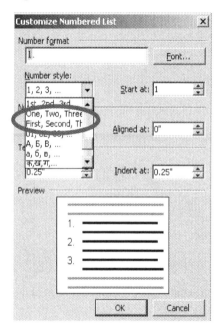

4.1.2 Instructions

I do not know about you, but I get tired of saying the same old thing a million times. Instead of repeating we can easily create a family point of reference with important information.

- Get a 3-ring binder, which will become the family's new reference binder.
- Next think of all the things you have to repeatedly say to your kids such as microwave instructions for leftovers, phone numbers for Grandma, instructions to make up the bed, instructions to properly sweep the kitchen, etc.
- Start creating documents for the binder. An example would be "Microwave Instructions for John".
- In a blank document, type a title such as "How Long to Microwave" or "How to sweep the kitchen" and press the enter key to proceed down to the next line or two.
- Type your instructions step by step and have the entire family add important pages to the binder.

Figure 9

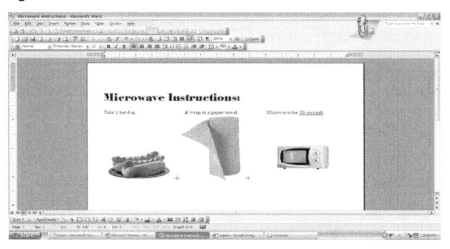

Note: If you would like to add pictures you can do so as described in the next example. Pictures are always a nice addition to wordy details. How best to sweep the kitchen to get the corners may be better portrayed with images. Would you rather describe or show how to properly clean the refrigerator? So the next time your kids need to know how to do something while you are at work or you are trying to wind down from work, they would independently refer to the reference binder of these documents instead of asking you over and over again. Another idea is to take a photo of the before and after you have cleaned a room so they can use for comparison when cleaning.

If you really want them to get into it then keep the digital camera close to the kitchen and have the family take pictures of each other the next time they microwave something or complete a chore. Then comeback and add *their* photographs to the instructions. In the office; is a reference binder not a great tool for employees?

4.1.3 Door Signs

My kids love this one. Let them create a document with their message and add a picture. For example: John's Room. My son and daughter both created their own signs. I did not think much of it other than I wanted to start teaching them computer skills. However, everyone loved them when they came for visits and my kids were so proud. "Proud of officially kicking each other out of each other's rooms". Every other day there was a new cleverer one. I remember one said "No Ashley's allowed" because the previous "No one over 9 allowed" prevented one of John's friends from entering his room.

However, you can create a no smoking, over 21 only, mom's closet – stay out sign, etc. Okay enough already, here is how to create the door sign:
- Type the details on the document as shown in Figure 10.
- Then change your font size by **selecting** your text and [clicking] the **Format** menu and then **Font**.
  IMPORTANT: when you want to change the font of certain words, **select** them by [clicking] your mouse and dragging over the text first.
- Then **choose** the formatting such as Bold, Size 24, etc. If you do not select the text that the program should make appear in Bold, then it does not have a clue what to make Bold.
- Change your Font Style, Size, and Color as you would like and [click] ok.
- Then [click] the **Format** Menu and **select** **Paragraph** (hence we want to center the paragraph on the page).

- Change your alignment to Center and [click] ok.
- Now move your mouse pointer to the location you want to insert a picture and click one time.
- [Click] **Insert** on the menu,
- [Click] **Picture**,
- [Click] **"From File"**.
- [Click] **Browse** and find the photo on your computer and [click] it as shown in Figure 11.

Figure 11

Note: You must know where you have stored the photo on your computer. A good place is in your "My Pictures" folder.

- Once you [click] the photo; [click] the **Insert** button. *(You may also simply double click the photo)*.
- With the picture now in your document, position your mouse pointer on the bottom right corner of your photo. [Click] and hold the left mouse button on that corner and drag the corner inward to reduce the size of the photo or outward to increase the size. You may need to try it a couple of times to get the hang of it.

Figure 12

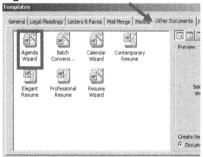

The family can even create seasonal and holiday signs to decorate their doors. The kids get so creative.

4.1.4   Vacation Agenda

Okay, let us face it

Figure 13

everyone wants to be a part of the vacation planning. Get together in a family meeting and document the planning in an agenda format using a Word document. Use the bullet style discussed earlier to create a checklist. Better yet, use the Agenda Wizard in the Templates tab to guide you as shown in Figure 13.

- Just [click] on **File**, then **New**.

- From the Task Pane located on the right side of the screen, [click] "**On my computer**" from the TEMPLATES section.
- [Click] the **Other Documents** tab. See Figure 12.
- [Click] **Agenda Wizard**.
- The wizard will guide you through a series of questions or inputs. Just add your information as requested and [click] next until you reach the Finish button. Fill in the document with the things you all would like to do on vacation. Now you have added some organization and a quick printable reference to use during vacation.

4.1.5 Dinner Menus

It is time for the kids to get fancy with the dinner. Choose one day out of the month to do a restaurant style dinner. Each month this can become a great family activity. Another thing you can do is allow the family to create the menu of courses and submit it for your approval. Can you just imagine when the in-laws come over for dinner?

- Open to a blank document and type the word "Menu".
- Then type the name of the Restaurant – The JJAQ Cuisine, I am using each member's initials for my example. Does it sound French???
- Then start the menu with an appetizers section, on to the main course, then dessert, etc. You can make it contemporary and then on the next occasion make it elegant. An example may be "Main Course features Homemade Italian Spaghetti with spicy home-made meatballs in a fresh tomato basil marinara sauce", aka Ragu.

Figure 14

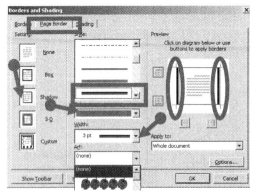

- Once all of the food items are listed then add a border by [clicking] **Format** (hence you are changing the look), then [click] **Borders and Shading**.
- <u>Select</u> the page border tab.
- Find and **<u>select</u>** the setting you like and style of choice.
- Then use the **preview area** to indicate which sides of the page should and shouldn't have borders as circled in Figure 14. A simple [click] of the border is all that is needed to add and delete from the page. The same goes for the top and bottom when working in the

preview section. My menu will only have side borders as shown in the preview.

- [Click] ok when done.

4.1.6 Event Program

Are your kids in the choir or band? Sometimes your kids want to show off their newly acquired talents when the family plans a gathering. Ask your kids to create a flyer for the event or a program style handout for invitees. If one wants to sing for Grandpa then you know the other(s) will also want to show Grandpa some type of talent/skill. If broad enough, the programs can be reused whenever a new performance is sparked.

Figure 15

- Open a blank document and type the title of the program (Humphries Talents).
- Then use the bullets to highlight different events such as Ashley . . . Piano Solo, John . . . Guitar Rock.
- In larger gatherings create a program of options. Billiards downstairs in the Basement, Swimming out back in the Pool, Video Games in John's Room (these can be broken out by Game and Time Slots for serious gamers), Dessert at 6pm on the deck.

Just have fun with the family and be creative.

4.2 Reports

4.2.1 Fax Cover Page

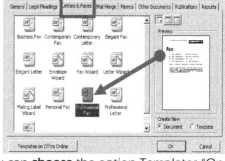

Figure 16

Fax templates are also available and are great for work as well.

- Just [click] **File** on the menu.
- Then [click] **New.**
- From the Task Pane on the right side of the screen, [click] **"On my computer"** located in the **TEMPLATES** section.
  Note: If you have a connection to the Internet you can **choose** the option Templates "On my Websites".
- The Templates box opens.
- [Click] the **Letters and Faxes** tab in the Template box.
- [Click] a Fax style that you prefer.
- [Click] the OK button.

4.2.2 Printable Calendar

Create a family calendar that can be posted in a central place for viewing.

- Simply use the built in template as we did with the fax earlier. See section 4.2.1.
- [Click] on **File, New,** then **select** "On my computer" from the Templates section of the Task Pane (right side of screen).
- Find the tab labeled "**Other Documents**" and **select** the **Calendar wizard**. It will guide you through the creation of the calendar.

Print and distribute to your family to update.

4.2.3 Newsletter

Help your extended family stay abreast of your family's yearly activities by designing an annual newsletter. Be sure to get the cousins involved. Each family member can be a journalist of a specific section of the newsletter. It is really a great thing to do around the New Year's holiday. Here is how to do it.

- Start a blank document.
- Then [click] on the **Insert** menu and <u>**select**</u> Text Box. Notice a **Create your drawing here** box appears along with your mouse pointer appearing as a black cross. The cross lets you draw your box when you [click] and drag your mouse.

Figure 17

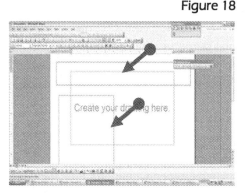

- Using your mouse click and drag to draw text boxes in a layout arrangement you think you would like your newsletter to follow as shown in Figure 17. Start with a Title Text Box at the top. Every newsletter should have the title should it not?
- Then repeat the Insert, Text Box steps until you have enough boxes drawn. This will include a couple of boxes for stories, Headings, etc.

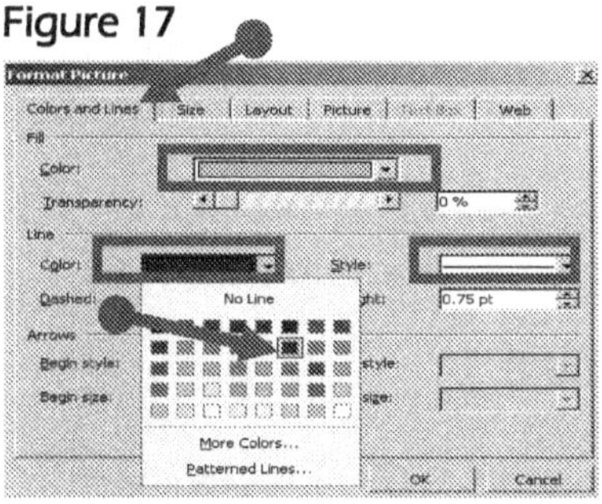

Note: I draw my boxes outside of the "Create your drawing here area", which is just a canvas to guide you. You can draw yours in or out of the canvas area.

Figure 18

To change the look of your textbox simply double [click] on one of the box border lines. Change the box **fill color** (background color) to a color such as light blue. Change the lines to a different color, thickness, or even set them to no lines. See Figure 18.

Additionally, you can [click] once on the line of a text box and from the Format menu, <u>**select**</u> **Text direction** to change the orientation of the words. See Figure 19.

Figure 19

- Each year your kids will be able to take on more responsibility of the newsletter and more family members may want to get involved before the final distribution. Do not forget to add photos. From the **Insert** menu, <u>**select**</u> **Pictures** "from file", and **browse** like earlier in Section 4.1.3 . This may take practice so start early.

4.2.4 Brochures

Your family can create a brochure about fun things to do at your home or to do in your area of town. When the kids have stay over friends, slumber parties, or even when you all have to accommodate out of town relatives this will prove very enlightening and resourceful.

- Open your templates box on your computer (refer to Section 4.2.1 for instructions to open Templates) and **select** the **Publications** tab then **Brochure**.
- Follow the directions on your computer.

The brochure is truly a nice alternative to a printed 8 ½ by 11 presentation handout. I have used brochures a number of times in the office to deviate from a boring 8 ½ by 11 document.

4.2.5 Vacation Report

Encourage your children to create a summary of their most memorable parts of this year's vacation. Each year you all can look back and recap. Keep them in a scrapbook for fun. Then when it is time for the annual newsletter they can reflect on the most important details to share with the family.

4.2.6 Print Screens

This technique can be applied to any document, but is especially handy for creating your instructions. A Print Screen button can be compared to a camera button. When pressed, it will capture a shot of your current screen view.

- To create a print screen (hence a capture of what is currently displayed on the screen) simply [click] your "Print Screen" button usually located towards the top right of your keyboard near the Home and Delete buttons. It in essence snaps a shot like a camera. Some computers may require an additional button such as shift to be pressed simultaneously with the print screen button.
- To Insert the print screen image into your document simply place your cursor in the document by [clicking] your mouse and then [click] **Edit** on the menu and **select** **Paste**. A shortcut for paste is to press Ctrl + V on your keyboard.

- Your image will appear. You can change some of the aspects by double [clicking] the image.
- **Select** the Layout tab and **choose** a wrapping style. **In line with text** is a good one to start off with.
- **Choose** a horizontal alignment (maybe center).
- Do not forget about the resize technique where you [click] the corner handle of the image and drag inward/outward.

Not only have I used this feature at work to create instructions for employees, but also to create instructions for myself while I was learning my job or new computer programs.

Figure 20

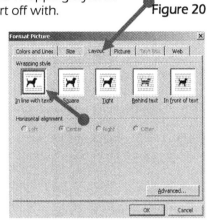

23

4.3 Proposals

4.3.1 Friend Info Form

Your children may enjoy creating a standard questionnaire to get to know their friends.
- Start with a blank document.
- Have them just start typing questions such as:
  - What is your favorite color?
  - What movie made you cry?
  - How many homeruns can you hit in a year?
  - What kind of car do you wish your Dad drove?
  - What do you eat when you go to the Olive Garden?
  - Etc.
- Keep it brief to encourage people to complete them. Make sure you have a place for Name, Birth date, and Address so the kids can keep in touch. Maybe even including Mom's name and cell phone will help you at times. I know sometimes I have to hunt my kids down.
- Now if you are creating a family questionnaire then it may be a good idea to break it down into sections such as about you and about your immediate family. Then you can get some great details about the family tree.

4.3.2 Compromise Contract

Figure 21

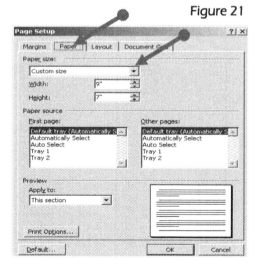

You should create an agreement/contract that outlines behavioral expectations and rewards/consequences for the behavior. Each party signs when an agreement is made. An example would be an allowance contract stating that if all chores are completed timely and school work done as instructed then an allowance of a certain amount will be issued bi-weekly. FYI – works great with your hubby too.

4.3.3 Gift Certificates/Spousal Coupons

Create stay up late coupons, snack coupons to mediate the number of snacks eaten, go to the park coupons, special hubby privileges coupons, etc. This is simple.

- Go to the **File** menu so we can change the size of the document.
- [Click] on **Page Setup** and then open the tab labeled Paper.
- **Choose** a new Paper size; postcard will work well or **choose** custom and enter the paper size.
- Create the wording for your coupon.
- Print and cut accordingly.
- Distribute as warranted

Figure 22

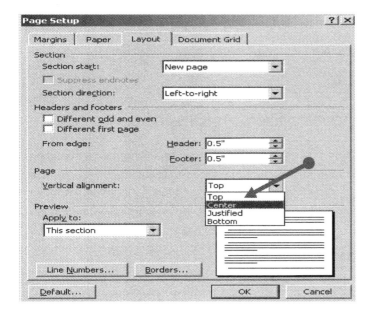

4.4 Homework

4.4.1 Cover Pages

This seems easy enough, but some people do not know the easiest way to accomplish this task. When your children have an assignment for school make sure they include a cover page with the title centered both horizontally and vertically. Leave the guess work out and let the program do it for you.

- On a blank page simply type the title on a line and then their name on another.
- The easiest way to center the typed data vertically on the page is to open the **File** menu, then Page Setup, and then the Layout tab.
- **Select** Vertical Alignment and **choose** center.
- No matter how many lines you add to the cover page it will center vertically on the page.
- Make sure you **select** the text and [click] the center alignment button on the toolbar also. This is for the horizontal centering.

4.4.2 Brainstorming Exercises (Org chart)

This strategy helps to organize thoughts for creating sentences and/or paragraphs. The idea is to start with a general topic that breaks down into 3 or more related thoughts. Although my example is about thinking of ideas to write a paper on sharks, you can use this to create ideas for the family. Some ideas may include brainstorming about vacation ideas, saving money, things to have at a birthday party. Help your children create a chart prior to their birthday about the type of party they want.

Figure 23

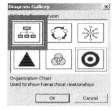

Figure 24

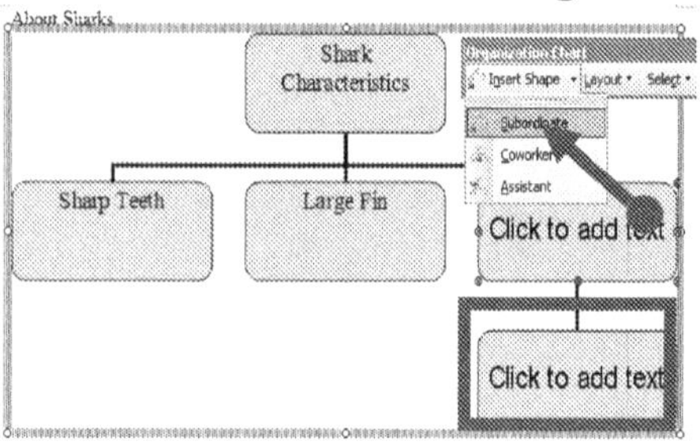

In this exercise we want to insert something into our document.

- [Click] on the **Insert** menu, [click] on **Diagram**.

- Then [click] on the organizational chart type (1st one). A pre-designed chart will load. However, you can **choose** any type of diagram that will work for your idea.
- [Click] Ok.
- Simply [click] a node (chart object) to add your information.
- If you [click] on a node, you can use the org chart menu to expand even further. Just [click] on **Insert Shape** and **choose** a **subordinate** for a node to appear below the selected node or coworker to add a peer node next to the box.

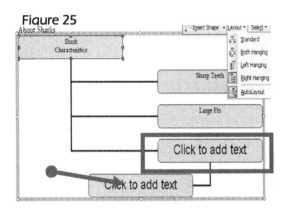

Figure 25

- To change the layout of the organizational chart simply [click] the Layout arrow on the Organizational Chart toolbar. In this case I chose Right Hanging. This idea is something you can actually use in the office too.
- Remember to **select** the node when applying changes. For instance, **select** the node that says Sharp Teeth to add a subordinate. Otherwise the program would not know where to add it.

4.4.3 Word Count and Other Statistics

Figure 26

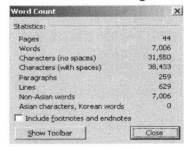

We all can think back to writing 500 words or more assignments or 250 words or less type of restrictions. So when your kids have a book report or document typed in Word they can check the word count by:

- **Selecting** the Tools menu and **choosing** Word count.

The word count dialog box will appear with the count details. I have also used the word count when I applied for jobs requesting a certain amount of words when summarizing my qualifications.

Not only can you track the number of words, but also the number of pages, paragraphs, lines, and more.

4.4.4 Dictionary

This is one of my favorite Tools because I never made the spelling bee.
- [Click] on a word you wish to have checked.
- Then [click] on the **Tools** menu.
- [Click] **Spelling and Grammar**.

Note: A shortcut would be to right [click] on a misspelled word to activate spelling or just press the F7 key.

4.4.5 Thesaurus

Here is another favorite that saves me from carrying around a heavy book.

Figure 27

- [Click] on the word.
- Then [click] on the **Tools** menu.
- [Click] Language.
- Finally [click] Thesaurus.

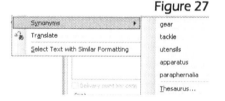

Your thesaurus will open in a pane to the right. A shortcut would be to right [click] and **<u>choose</u> Synonyms** or just press Shift + F7.

4.5 Labels

4.5.1 Mailing Labels

Creating mailing labels with your address is quick and easy. This is a tool so:

- [Click] on the **Tools** menu.
- Then [click] on **Letters and Mailings**

Figure 28

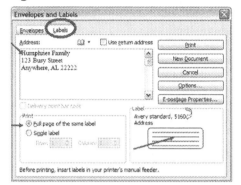

- [Click] **Envelopes and Labels**
- Open the Labels tab and type your information in the Address section.
- Now in the Print section make sure you **select** the Full page of the same label option.
- The Label section needs to be set to the appropriate label size according to the label paper you will print on. Normally, address labels that print 30 per page are the "**5160**" standard product.

Figure 29

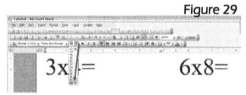

$$3x = \qquad 6x8=$$

- Just [click] on the label drawing to **select** other options.
- When you are done entering your information; [click] the **New Document** button.

My family has used labels for many different things including mass mailings.

Figure 30

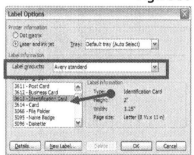

4.5.2 Flash cards

This is just another form of labels except we do not have to print to labeled paper. We will just print on regular paper and cutout. Let us repeat the steps for Labels (see previous tip).

- Then [click] on the Label section and **choose** Product number **5315** or any Note Card you would like. Make sure the Label products is set to Avery standard.
- [Click] Ok.
- Then [click] "New document".
- Before you start typing, change your **Font size to 72.**
- Note: **View** the ruler for positioning. If you do not see the ruler, [click] **View**, and then [click] **Ruler**. You will see the ruler shown in Figure 31.

Figure 31

4.5.3 Recipe Cards

This is your opportunity to create recipe cards with actual photos of your decorated plates. Therefore, this is a must do for the rare occasions where I cook something that turns out beautifully. As the years go by, my cooking does get better.

Your hubby and kids can join in the fun as they cook too.

- Start your labels as described in the previous step.
- Instead of entering math problems simply type your recipes with a **Font** size of 12pts or so.
- However, you can add **Pictures** once you take some of your cooked recipes by [clicking] the **Insert** menu.
- Then [click] **Picture From File".**
- Find your **Picture** by browsing.
- When found, [click] the Insert button.

Figure 32

4.5.4 ID Badge

A great idea for very informal dinner parties is to create imaginative badges and have a meet and greet hour. Create some

Qwin Humphries
Mother
Microsoft Dabbler

D.O.B
02/16/74

of these for your guests and include something interesting about them that they would not mind others knowing. If you do not have a photo of your guest, use web photos or clipart to represent them.

The identification badge also works like the mailing label. Open your Label maker as described earlier.

Figure 33

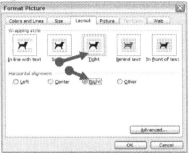

- Now [click] on the **Label** button so we can choose the label product. **Select** product number 3613 or any other Identification Card label.
- [Click] Ok
- Then [click] **New Document**.

Make sure you set your picture to the best size and layout. Just double [click] the picture and **select** the **Size** tab. You may want to change the percentage of the height by 50% or so. To Layout tab will allow you to position your picture on the left, center, right, or other.

4.5.5 Good Work/Hubby Stickers

Figure 34

I can remember the gold stars I got in 2nd grade for good work and behavior. Well this is a step up and can be used all around for the family and yourself. Let the kids make some to give you when you do a great mommy job.

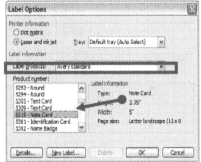

- Open your **Envelopes and Labels** tool (**Tools** menu).
- Then **choose** Avery **5160**.
- [Click] New Document.
- Start typing your Atta boys. Get personal and say "Excellent job son!" or "That's my honey!" or "You go girl!"

31

4.5.6 Location Labels

Label your drawers, shelves, or boxes. This time use the smaller return address labels. They are done the same exact way as the mailing label.

- Just enter your information in the Label box and **choose** the Return label product number.
- Then open in a new document.

There are 80 labels per page so these should last you quite awhile.

4.5.7 Locker Tabs

If you ever encounter a child that is tardy in school because of locker frustration then here is a tip for you. I would know from experience.

- Create labels in **Avery 5160** and open in a New Document. Remember to create enough for each book and binder. The blank labels can simply be saved for later or just go ahead type your child's name in them and use later for something else.
- Each label is going to have a number representing the number of times they visit their locker in a day. In my child's case this was 4 times.
- So we created labels from 1 – 4 all with a **Font** size of 36. Just create the 1st top Left label first, which will be copied over.
- **Select** everything in that label and **select** Edit on the menu and then **Copy**.
- Then [click] **Edit** again and **Paste**. (Ctrl + C is the copy shortcut while Ctrl + V is the paste shortcut).
- Then we added pictures to each label. Place your cursor in the location you would like your picture.
- [Click] the **Insert** menu.
- [Click] **Picture**
- [Click] **Clipart**.

Figure 35

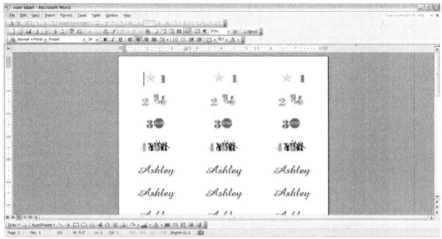

My daughter just stuck these labels on her school books and binders and was able to quickly pick up all relevant books by their periods. The less you have to think about when stopping by the locker between periods, the better.

However, this can be easily done for toddlers around the home.
- Make a label for the sock drawer with the word "Socks" and a picture of some socks.
- Then stick it on the drawer.

They will learn how to identify, read, and spell. Try it.

4.5.8 Gift Tags

These are great especially at Christmas or just for a special occasion such as when you give your hubby a sweet surprise.

- Just create your label in **Avery 5160** and open in a new document.
- Then **Insert** a "special" photo of yourself that suits the occasion. Remember to use the **Insert** menu and <u>select</u> **Pictures** and **From file**.
- Now for your kids, this is a different story.
- Have them take pictures in honor of the festivities such as putting on a Santa hat at Christmas.

- Then **Insert** their photo on the label and type something like: Season Greetings from Ash and John.
- People always love my gift tags because they get to keep a picture of the family. It is an inexpensive way to issue photos to everyone. I do not print them on adhesive paper, but glossy paper instead. It would be hard to peel sticky labels and put them in a photo album or scrapbook.

Figure 36

4.6 Personal

4.6.1 Business Cards

Figure 37

Here we go with the labels again.

- Open your **Tools** menu.
- [Click] **Mailings and Labels**.
- [Click] **Envelopes and Labels**.
- Then [click] on the label image located in the bottom right corner of the dialog box.
- **Select** product number **3612** which is the Business Card template.
- Now [click] ok to return to the Envelopes and Labels box.
- [Click] **New Document**. You will have a 2 x 10 page to create your business cards. Create enough for each of your children.
- **Insert** a picture from a file or just play around. These are also very nice for hubby play. You or he can be anyone!!!
- Highlight your information from the first card and [click] on **Edit** and then **Copy**.
- Then move to the right column for the second business card and [click] **Edit** and then **Paste**.

Figure 38

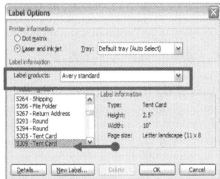

4.6.2 Place Card

While your kids may like to create a place card for their desk (John John's Office), you can create them for special occasions such as Thanksgiving Dinner. An example may be to place children at the table to organize an area to eat together.

- Once again **select** Tools and go to **Labels**.

- <u>Select</u> Label 5309.
- Create in a New Document.
- Think about the printed document being folded.
- That would mean that the top portion of the paper would actually end up as the back when folded. The bottom would display the

Figure 39

Qwin Humphries
Instructor

name. So tab down to the bottom portion and enter the text for the place card. See Figure 39.

4.6.3 Greeting Card

We all know about greeting cards so here is the how to.

- Open your Word to a blank document.
- Now change the page layout to landscape (longer width) by [clicking] **File** and then **Page Setup**.
- [Click] **Landscape** in the Orientation section.
- Then you need to change the document into a two-column document. One side is for the back and one for the front. So [click] **Format** (hence changing the look) and [click] **Columns**.
- Then [click] the **two column** image. If you would like you can <u>select</u> the "line between" checkbox to create a center line. Notice Figure 40 shows the page ruler splitting the page into two equal columns.
- Now since we want to start our text in the second column let us **Insert** a column break to help us by pass adding blank lines in the first column. <u>Select</u> Insert – **Break** – **Column break**.
- Create the front of your card. When done, **Insert** another column break. Create the left inner side of your card and then the right. **Print**!

Figure 40

4.6.4 Invitation

Figure 41

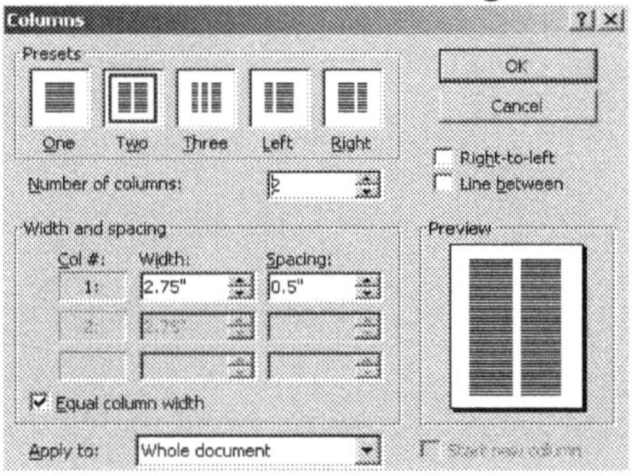

Set up the same as in the previous step for Greeting Card.

- Open a Word document.
- Set the page setup to landscape orientation.
- Then **Insert** two columns.
- In the first column type up your invitation with any pictures you would like to insert.
- Then highlight everything in the column and [click] **Edit** on the menu and then **Copy.**
- Now insert a column break as described in the previous step.
- In the 2nd column [click] **Edit** on the menu and select **Paste.**

There you have it. Print as many as you need.

5 Can I Excel in this?

Many people find this application complicated to use so I will do my best to break it down before going into any ideas. Try to imagine of an account ledger such as your checkbook register. Your checkbook register is equivalent to a workbook. You open it up to the sheet where you would record your banking transactions: "ABC Grocery, $85"; etc. The sheets inside are the worksheets where your transactions are recorded. As with the checkbook you have rows and columns to identify the information for your transactions.

Microsoft Excel® opens in what is called a work**book**, which by default has 3 work**sheets** but can have more worksheets added or deleted at anytime *(not so important for our usage)*. The most important thing to grasp is that every row and column in a worksheet has an interception or meeting point called a "REFERENCE LOCATION". So the first box you see on your worksheet (by the way the official name for the box is called a "cell") is located horizontally/across row "1" and vertically/down column "A". You would refer (hence "reference") that box or cell as "A1". I do not want to take you back to Algebra and graphing (x,y) so I will use the example of an auditorium for relating reference location.

Figure 42

You purchase a ticket for you, your husband and your kids to see Disney on Ice. Okay, I may be lame. Your husband is going to meet you there after work and has his ticket. Unlike me, you have decent seats outside of the nosebleed section at G36, G37, G38, and G39. Why is the letter and number so significant??? So you can tell if you will be sitting with your family of course. Secondly, *you* need to make it to your seat. You must make your way to section "G" (our **column** section in Microsoft Excel®) and find the row with the 30's (our Microsoft Excel® **row**) within that "G" section. Then you have to find those 4 consecutive seats within the 30's row. The logic is the same with worksheets. We find the location and enter something into those cells. Can you find G39 on the worksheet? We obviously need to know how to communicate to our computer as well as others where something is located just as the ticket master lets us know where we are sitting. Your ticket is not going to say "sit over there".

In addition to location, another important concept to grasp is the three different types of **CELL CONTENT**.

1. **LABEL** (Identification –since your check register is designed for the purpose of listing your transaction it has labels preprinted on the sheets. An example would be [Date], [Amount], [Payee], etc. Since Microsoft Excel® isn't always used for a check register; you would need to enter this information into the worksheet. So if you enter the words "CHECK AMOUNT" into the 1st cell – A1; then just below it in the next cell you would start entering your 1st amount of $80 and repeat those steps as many times as necessary. When you look back and see $80 you will know it is the **amount** of a written check.

2. **DATA** (Information – this would be the actual date, amount, and so forth).

3. **FORMULA** (Calculation – to distinguish to the Microsoft Excel® application that you wish for it to compute something for you, you must enter an equal, **=,** sign into the cell prior to typing anything. You are alerting the application to <u>equal</u> something for you instead of just labeling. After typing **=**, you can then enter numbers such as =2+2 and then [click] the enter button on your keyboard and it will display the computed result of 4. However, that is not the most efficient way to use the application as you will see in some of my ideas within this chapter. The best way to get acquainted and comfortable to the functionality is to try and practice.

5.1 Checklists

Figure 43

5.1.1 Guest List

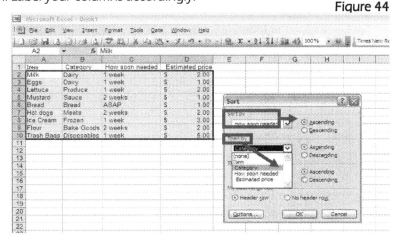

- Open Microsoft Excel®
  and label four columns
  accordingly:
  - A1: Name,
  - B1: Phone,
  - C1: RSVP,
  - D1: Date.

Note: When you [click] on the cell with the label "Name", the row and column highlight in orange to indicate your position. Also the location or address of that cell is shown as A1. See Figure 43.

- Now let us start listing the information /data/ for each guest starting at row 2. The labels help us and others know what the data represents. Just type the name, phone numbers, reservation status, and date for each invitee.

5.1.2 Grocery List

Just as with the guest list you can create a grocery list and so can your children. Label your columns accordingly:

Figure 44

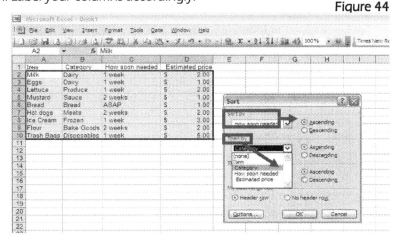

A1: Item, B1: Category, C1: How soon needed, D1: Estimated price.

- Then simply enter your groceries as needed.
- When you are ready to shop, you should sort and sum your list. **Select** all of the cells in your list by [clicking] cell **A2**.
- Then hold down the Shift key on your keyboard and [click] the last cell in your list. Mine would be **D10**. (All cells A1 through D10 should now be selected. Alternatively you can [click] and drag your mouse to select).
- Then [click] the **Data** command on the menu.
- [Click] **Sort**.
  - The sort box will appear. In this case I need everything marked as needed in 1 week listed first and then in the order of category so I do not wander around the grocery store wasting time. The longer I stay in the store the more dangerous it is to my purse. In **Sort by choose** "How soon needed" – **Ascending**.
  - In the **Then by choose** "Category" – **Ascending**.
- Next let us add up the estimated cost of the groceries. Since the grand total will display in E2, *(Note the orange highlighted areas column E and row 2)* we must first enter an equal sign in the E2 cell to alert the application to compute something.

Figure 45

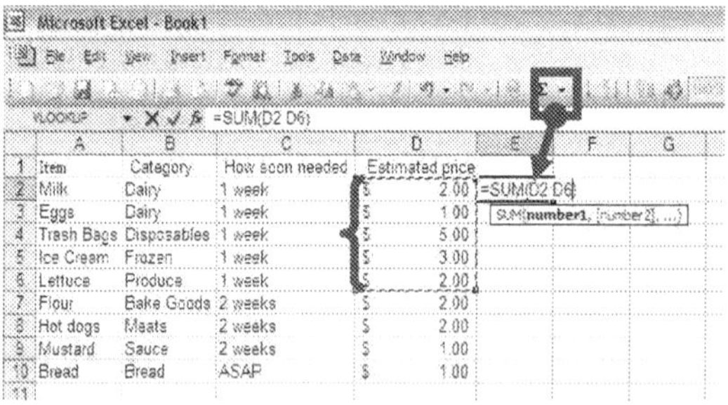

- Then [click] the drop arrow of the **Autosum** button, which looks like a backwards letter E and **choose Sum**. (Note: when using the Autosum feature it is not necessary to type the = sign into the cell).
- A thick white plus sign appears as your cursor *(this sign means you can **select** cells)*.
- [Click] on the first price and while still holding the mouse button, scroll down to the last price for week 1, which is located in cell E6. Release the mouse button and [click] the enter key.
- There you have it. You may have to practice a couple of times to get the hang of it. There are several ways to **select** cells, but this is a great way to start.

5.1.3 School Supplies

Create a school supply list in the same manner you did with the grocery list except you can leave out the how soon needed column. You may want to replace it with a "For Whom" if you have more than one child. This would also be nifty if you are keeping a running tab over a period of time.

5.1.4 Behavior Chart

Figure 46

Create this chart by starting the following columns: *A1: Behavior, B1: Violation Date, C1: Initials*

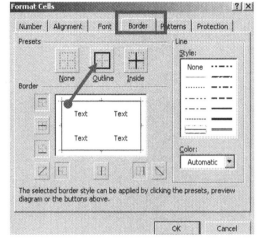

You will need some grid lines so this chart can be printed and updated on the hard copy. What good is a behavior chart unless the participants can see it and know that everyone else can too?

- **Select** the columns that should have grids by holding the Ctrl key on the keyboard and [clicking] on the *letter* of each column. These letters are called Column Headings. Make sure you [click] the column letters A, B, and C.
- If you experience trouble, simply [click] on A of the first column and without releasing the [click] move your mouse right until you reach column D. Dragging is an alternative to the Ctrl and [click].
- To create your grids, [click] on **Format** (hence changing the look).
- Then [click] **Cells**.
- Then [click] on the Borders tab.
- [Click] the outline box under Presets. The Border section should update to show a line drawn on each side. You can also change the style of the line to make it a dash or make it thicker or change the color.

- [Click] ok when finished.
- Print and post around the house.

5.1.5 Chores

I do not know about you, but sometimes detailing the actual process to "properly" complete chores comes in handy. For instance, cleaning the bathroom encompasses cleaning the sink, sweeping the floor, cleaning the tub, cleaning the toilet, etc. So why not create a chore checklist in a spreadsheet? You can create one for the families' routine chores.

- Start your worksheet as we did before and just list the label in each column. **A1: Chore, B1: Day of the Week, C1: Check When Done**.
- Complete accordingly.

Figure 47

	A	B	C
		ALLOWANCE VIOLATION	
1			
2	**NAME:**		
3	**DATE:**		
4			
5	CHECK	DESCRIPTION	COST
6		UNMADE BED	$ 0.50
7		ROOM CLUTTER	$ 1.00
8		MISSED CHORE	TBD
9		SCHOOL WORK	1 DAY'S TY
10		ATTITUDE	$ 1.00
11		TALKING BACK	$ 0.50
12		DISRESPECTFUL	1 DAY'S TY
13		GROOMING RELATED	$ 0.50
14		MISSED BATH	$ 1.00
15		LEAVING ITEMS AROUND HOUSE	$ 0.50
16		LATE WORK	TBD
17		INCONSIDERATE	TBD
18		OTHER	TBD
19			
20	DETAILS:		
21			
22			
23			
24			
25			
26			

5.1.6 Allowance Violation

Let us face it. As parents we are the police patrol, judge, warden, etc. I know when I tell my kids that they have not done a chore or that they are slacking with the school lesson; they seem to think I am going overboard. So I thought I would try documenting it *(as we sometimes do at work)* to let them see how many times they actually do those things. Let us create a violation ticket where we can print them to check off whenever we see a violation and eventually issue a ticket. Consider yourself the hallway patrol.

- **Select** a Font you would like to work with by [clicking] the **Font Type** arrow on the toolbar and scrolling down the list until you select the one you would like to use in the spreadsheet.

- Change the size if you would like. I used a Copperplate 14pt.
- Create your worksheet with a title in A1.
- Follow the format in Figure 47 if you prefer or create your own set of violations. We will add the background and colored text next.
- **Select** the cells you would like to display a background color.
- Then **select** the background fill button on the toolbar. (If you do not see it then [click] the Toolbar Options arrow as shown in Figure 48.
- **Select** **Add or Remove Buttons**.
- **Select** **Formatting** (deals with the look).
- Then find the toolbar button that resembles a tilted bucket of color. [Click] it. This is the fill tool.

Figure 48

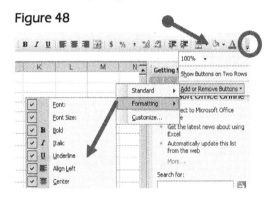

- Now with those cells still selected, [click] the fill button's drop arrow to open the color palette.

5.2 Budgeting

Okay, this is a hard topic to implement, but we all need to do it.

5.2.1 Calendar Dates

Microsoft Excel® allows you setup sequential dates pretty easily because it recognizes patterns.

- From a new worksheet, enter the starting date in A1. I will use 1/1/07 as an example.
- **Select** column heading letter A.
- [Click] on the **Format** menu and [click] Cells.
- On the Number tab [click] **Date** in the *Category* section and in the *Type* section find a style that suits your need.
- I like to show the day of the week and the date so I selected that format.
- [Click] ok when done.
- Move your mouse pointer to the very right bottom corner of that cell **until the pointer/cursor changes into a black plus sign "+".** This symbolizes your drag and fill indicator. (Hence a thick white plus sign is your **select** indicator while the move indicator is denoted by a thin plus sign with arrows pointed at each end).

Figure 49

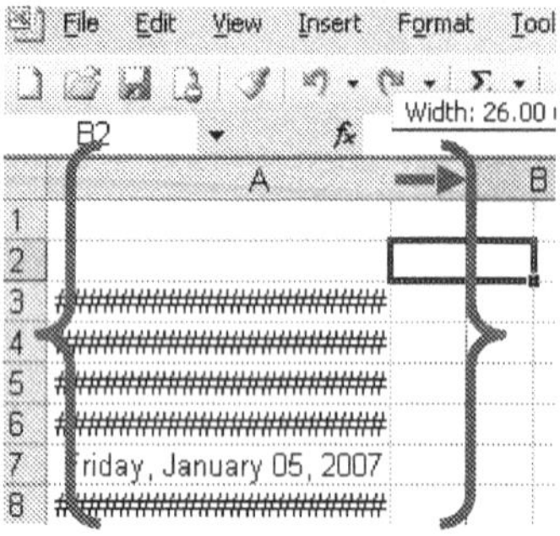

- If your cells end up with number signs this just means there is not enough room to display the results. Simply expand your column by [clicking] the right line border in the top gray section (column heading) and dragging right as shown in Figure 49. In this case that would be the line between letters A and B.
- Double [click] the border to auto resize or just [click] and drag to manually resize.

5.2.2 Family Calendar

This spreadsheet should also display a list of dates, but this time we want to have a title displayed at the top. So we have to make room for a title before we can insert one.

Figure 50

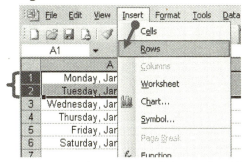

- Continuing from the previous tip, **Insert** 2 rows at row 1.
- Remember to **select** rows 1 and 2 so that the program knows where to place the 2 inserted rows. (See Figure 50).
- Then [click] **Insert** on the menu and then **select** **Rows**.
- Enter your family members starting in Row 2 and Column B.
- Then resize the columns so that you can view all of your details inside the cells.
- **Select** the gray column letters B – E. If you have more or less family members than me then **select** everyone's column. We want to change the width of the columns so [click] **Format** and **Columns** then **Width**.

Figure 51

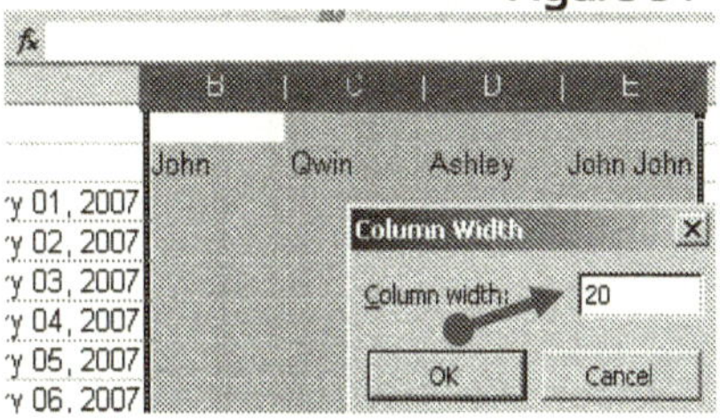

- Enter **30** in the column box that appears and [click] ok.
- While you still have the columns selected let us program the cells to wrap our data so we can maintain the column width at all times even though we can have a bit of text in them. This means the row height will adjust to the data we enter while the column width remains intact. Reselect the columns if necessary and [click] the **Format** menu.
- [Click] **Cells**.

Figure 52

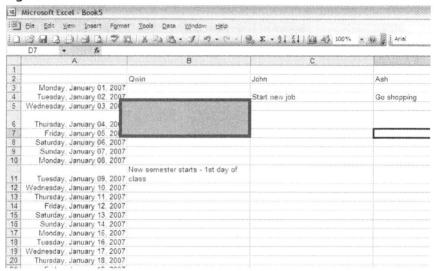

- Now go to the alignment tab and check the box located towards the bottom named **Wrap Text**.
- [Click] ok.
- You may now just start typing in each member's schedules. When you type data that requires multiple lines to display the rows will automatically resize. Use this idea as a place to see everyone's schedule at once. You can actually save it and email as an attachment to each member.

5.2.3 Family Budget

One of the best places to start a family budget is in a spreadsheet. List your family expenses and income to monitor your spending and saving habits. Sometimes it may show your bad habits such as . . . SHOPPING. This time we will stay in the same workbook as the Family Calendar and just start on Sheet 2 of the workbook.

- First open your Family Calendar if you already have not done so or feel free to start a new worksheet if you did not do that exercise.

- Name your worksheet by double [clicking] on the **Sheet 2** tab located towards the bottom left corner of the screen.
- Type the name of your sheet as shown in the Figure 53.
- Start with a Title in cell A1 of this new worksheet. Type something to the effect of Family Budget.

Figure 53

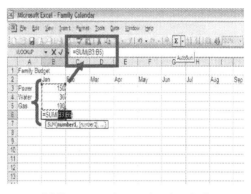

- Then in Row 2 and starting in column B **(B2)** start typing in the months; stop at the 2nd month so we can just drag as we did with the calendar dates. (Remember to just drag patterns to make them auto populate).
- Now **select** the two months you entered in B2 and C2 – in my case Jan. and Feb.
- Then scroll your mouse pointer to the right corner of the C2 cell until the black plus symbol appears. The corner of the cell contains a tiny black square called a handle.
- [Click] that corner handle while the black cross symbol displays and pull to the right until you reach the month Dec. (or whatever month you would like to end your budget). As you move to the right a text indicator will pop in and out to show you the month that will appear in that cell. For this example I just stopped at Dec.

Figure 54

- Release your mouse.
- Now start entering your fixed expenses in column A starting at A3. Then after you have entered all expenses [click] in the cell just below the last row's expense.
- [Click] the **Autosum** button (the backwards E symbol) and if the range of cells are captured in the selection then [click] ok.

- Finally let us update the calculation to perform for each month by **selecting** the right corner handle of the cell we just performed the Autosum in and dragging over to Dec's column.
- Note: If you need to add more expenses later you can **select** the rows where you would like that data to be placed as long as they are within that calculated range and **Insert** rows. The calculated results will automatically include them as well as long as they fall within the area of the initial range.
- An example would be having a Grand Total in D4 that sums cells D1 through D3. When I discover I left out an expense I would select row 3 and insert a row. D4 would then move down to D5 and automatically sum D1 through D4.

5.2.4 Allowance Schedule

Figure 55

This one is great for the kids. If they are old enough get them to set it up and you approve it. They can really see how their allowance will add up if saved or what they will be missing if they do not earn their allowance for a week or two.

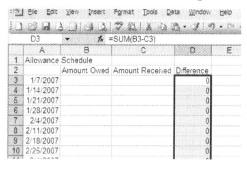

- Open a new spreadsheet.
- At the top in cell **A1** type the title – **Allowance Schedule**.

Figure 56

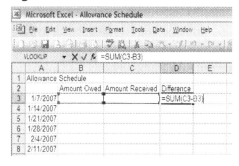

- Then in Row 2 starting in Cell **B2**, type the label **Amount Owed**. Then in **C2** enter **Amount Received**.
- In **D2** enter the heading **Difference**.
- Now enter the first pay date in cell A3

and the second pay date in A4 (hence we are starting a pattern that we want the program to repeat). It even picks up on a weekly pattern as shown in Figure 55.

- **Select** those two dates that make up the pattern.
- Move your mouse pointer to the right corner of the 2nd pay date's cell, which should be located in A4 until you see the black cross that resembles a plus sign "+". Note, both dates must still be selected.
- [Click] the right corner handle of the bottom cell *(a small black square)* and drag down until you the ending date you would like flashes. You can always add more dates to the spreadsheet later.
- The program assumes you want the repeat the weekly pattern of the 2 cells you selected and adds dates for each week. If you pay allowances bi-weekly or the 1st and 15th you can simply enter those dates and then **select** and drag the pattern as described above.

Figure 57

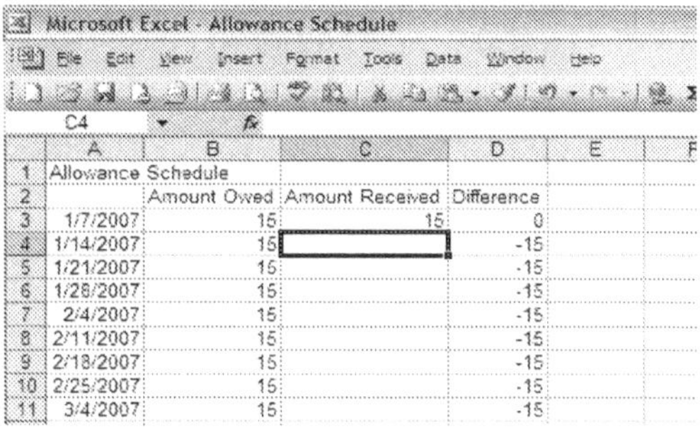

- If you would rather type in the dates manually that is fine as well.
- Finally, create a formula to calculate the difference in column D. In D3 type the following: **=SUM(C3-B3)**. That indicates to the application to **total** or sum **whatever is in cell C3 and subtract whatever is in B3**.

Note: the formula does not contain any blank spaces.

5.3 Charts

5.3.1 Sports League Scorecard

Figure 58

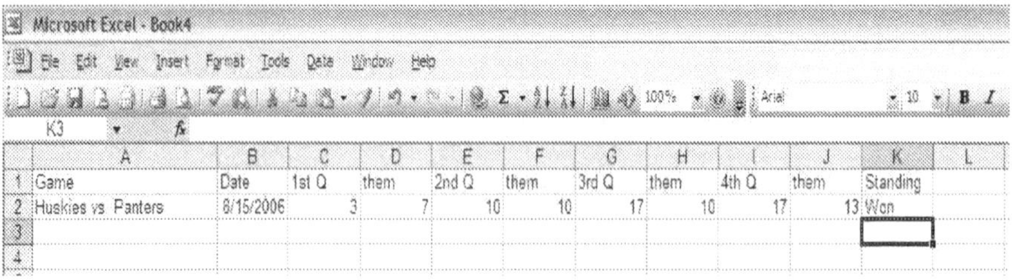

Create a spreadsheet that has **Game, Date,** and **Q1, them, Q2, them, Q3, them, Q4, them,** and **Standing** columns. You can create 9 endings if you are working on baseball; change it for bowling, etc. Once you have entered your labels, begin entering your scores in the cells below.

If you would like a simple graph just **select** a name column and the scores. Then press the **F11 key**.

5.3.2 Voting Ballot

Type a questionnaire that can be computed to give results. I have seen the magazine short quizzes where I scored my answers between 1 – 5 and tabulated the final score to see where I stood as a fashion guru. This is that same type of idea and would be a fun activity for the hubby. Just start in cell A1 and type Questions for the label. Then in Cell B1 type: Answer 1: yes, 2: maybe, 3: no. Then type your 10 to 20 question starting at A2. The person will simply answer each question by typing 1, 2, or 3 in the corresponding column B cell. After the quiz is completed, simply go use the AutoSum feature to tally the results. You may even want to use the average result in the Autosum drop down arrow.

5.3.3 Menu For The Month

Some people plan their meals in advance. I have tried this and even posted it to the web so my family could go online and view it. It was great to view and track how often I did not keep to the schedule. However, my issues do not have anything to do with how well it works for you. Try it out and you may like it. I liked it, but I would like it better if I wasn't the cook. Just create your dates for the month in column A. Then in column B, type your meals for those days. Print and post on the refrigerator or email to the family.

5.4 Homework

5.4.1 Graph Paper

Figure 59

- Simply open a blank spreadsheet and [click] **Ctrl** and the **A key** to highlight the entire worksheet.
- [Click] on the **Format** menu.

Figure 60

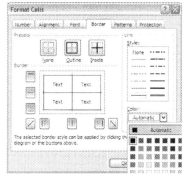

- Then [click] **Column**.
- Then [click] **Width**.
- Enter 2 for the new size and [click] ok as in Figure 59.
- Now make sure the columns are still selected or reselect if necessary and then [click] the **Format** menu, **Cells**, open the **Border** tab, then [click] **Outline** and **Inside**, then click ok. See Figure 60.

Figure 61

- Change your font color to white using your Font color button on the toolbar.
- Type a period in cell A1. Notice you will not see it due to the white coloring. 
- Right [click] cell A1 and **select** **Copy**.

- **Select** Edit on the menu and **choose** Select All.
- **Select** Edit on the menu and **choose** Paste.
- See the final result in Figure 61.

5.4.2 Self Multiplication Tester

Okay, it really takes time to teach your kids multiplication. Once they learn they still need a verification tool. So why not create a little system they can use themselves for independent study.

Figure 62

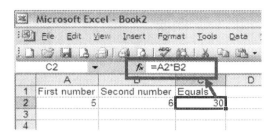

- Open a spreadsheet and label accordingly: A1: **First number,** B1: **Second number**, and C1: **Equals.**
- Then find the location where

you would like the answer stored such as in C2.

In C2, enter this formula: **=A2*B2** and press enter. So whatever is entered in A2 or B2 at all times will be multiplied and the result will display in cell C2. Note: you can change the operation instead of * you can divide by using the backslash "/" symbol. Your kids will probably need that one next. Also you may want to change the result font color to Red for easy spotting.

- Then once your kids have practiced this for a while, you can partner together and quickly test them yourself as an involved mother. Or if you need to buy time while you start dinner, just have them work on this. It's even great with older kids to use bigger numbers such as 25 x 8 = . . .

5.4.3 Powers That Be

Along the same lines as the self multiplication table or division table, the powers that be will prove handy when you need to wind down, but your kids need to prepare for math. This one helps them figure out the power of a number they enter in the First number column.

Figure 63

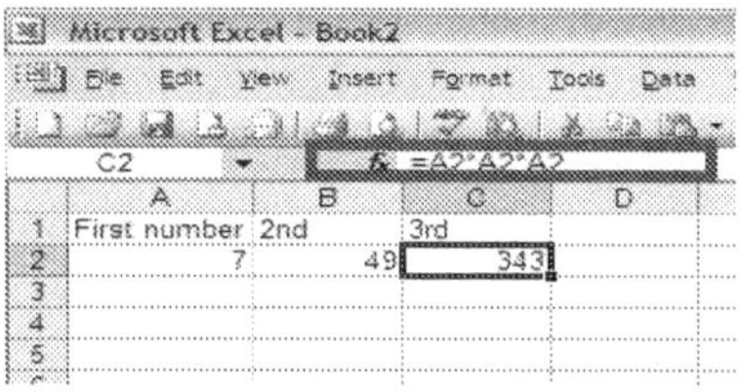

- Start your column headings as such; **A: First Number, B:**

55

2nd, C: 3rd.

- In cell B2 type the following: =A2*A2 and press enter.
- In cell C2 type the following: =A2*A2*A2 and press enter.
- Let me explain the way it works. Your child enters a number in cell A2.
- Then B2 will update with the 2nd power of the number.
- C2 will update with the 3rd power of the number. The result will display in the cell, however you can always see there is a formula computing behind the scene by looking at the formula bar up top.

5.4.4 Common Denominator (C/D)

Another great one that saves me by allowing me time to unwind and be focused by the time I get to my children's homework is the common denominator, C/D, idea. I remember my daughter had an assignment that took a while because she had to figure out whether or not there was a C/D. Well I came up with this one rather quickly to save my sanity and dignity.

- Type your columns: **A: Number, B: Factor, D: Try** (Number).
- Then in B2, type the following: =A2/D2 and press enter. You will see #DIV/0! (Meaning you cannot divide by zero). Until numbers are placed in cells A2 and D2 to actually be calculated you will get this error message. It is okay because the cell will automatically update once those numbers are entered. Note: The dollar signs mean absolute reference. No matter what or where we move or copy the formula, the contents will divide by whatever is entered in D2. D2 is now absolutely static or "absolute" in spreadsheet terms.

Figure 64

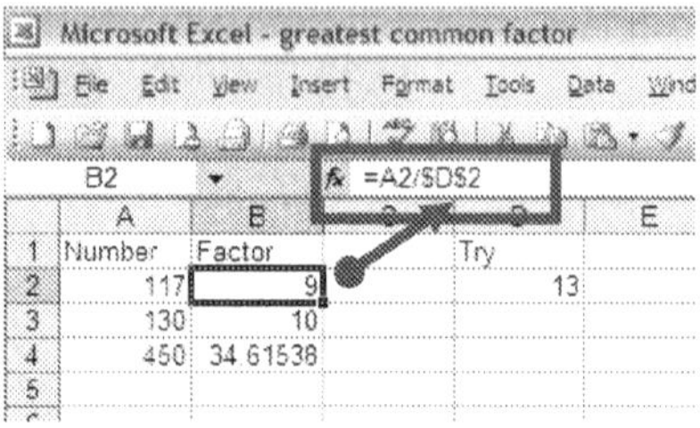

- Now **select** cell B2 and press copy (Ctrl + C or Edit and then Copy).
- Now **select** cells B3 and B4 and perform a paste (Ctrl + V). Since the absolute reference was established with D2, it remained part of the formula no matter where it was copied.

- The design is done and ready for use so let me clarify how it works. Your child should enter the main number in D2, and a number in the A2 cell.
- Then they would enter numbers to test in column A. If the factor is a whole number such as 10 rather than a decimal such as 10.6 then it is a denominator.

I hope this helps.

5.5 Directory

5.5.1 Family Tree

There is a really good way to do this one so that you later can import into another Microsoft program – Visio® the flow charting application. It will relate the information from the spreadsheet and draw out diagrams to visualize the flow. All you would have to do is

Figure 65

	A	B	C
1	Name	Position	Branch
2	Qwin Humphries	Mom	Jerry Coleman
3	Dave Robinson	Cousin	Net Williams
4	Jerry Coleman	Dad	Carrie Coleman
5	Net Williams	Aunt	Carrie Coleman
6	Cherita Goodson	Aunt	Carrie Coleman
7	Carrie Thomas	Aunt	Carrie Coleman
8	Charlie Coleman	Uncle	Carrie Coleman
9	Jerry Coleman III	Brother	Jerry Coleman
10			

import the spreadsheet into the program. However, until then it can be sorted and arranged within a spreadsheet.

- Start your labels in A1 – C1 as follows: **Name**, **Position**, and **Branch**.
- Then start filling out each row as you think of family members.
- The idea is to have several people associated with the same branch name. However, the branch must also have an extension until you reach the main (eldest) branch.

So my example shows I am a branch of my dad, Jerry Coleman, who is a branch of Carrie Coleman; my grandmother. Then there is another extension of Jerry Coleman who happens to be my brother Jerry III. The branch column contains two Jerry Coleman cells because he has two children. Now I would continue to add my two children under name and associate the Branch as me, Qwin Humphries. Though it can get confusing just think of it creating a person in the name column and their parent in the branch column. If they *(those listed in the name column)* have children, immediately create a new row for each of their children.

Believe it or not I have used this one on the job to create some superb organization charts. It was so much quicker than drawing and moving objects around. The only difference was the Branch column was the Manager column while the Name column was the Employee. So I reported to my manager who reported to her manager who reported to an even higher manager. Once I started the import the magic just happened.

5.5.2 Friends And Family Directory

Sometimes you just cannot find a long lost friend's number. Or maybe your kids have a play date, but do not have the phone numbers on hand. You know you will need all of the numbers including home, cell, mom's cell, dad's cell, etc. What about Aunt Challis and Uncle Obe who live in Fort Lauderdale or even Uncle Gus and the family? Do you have their home and cell phone numbers handy? Well now you will after completing this spreadsheet. If you want, you can categorize each family member's contacts by sheet tabs. However, it would be very easy to just add a column that specifies this detail.

Setup your spreadsheet with the **first name, last name, home phone, cell phone, address, city, state, zip, birth date,** and **comments**. Then just fill in accordingly.

5.6 Tracking and Timelines

5.6.1 Eating Diary/Journal

Figure 66

Open an empty spreadsheet. Then enter the name or heading you would like to track such as: **Date**, **Food**, **Food Type**, **Meal Time**, **Calories**, and **Carbs**. These names should go in Row 1,

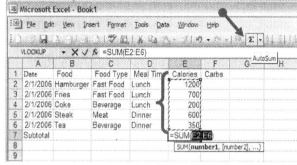

Columns A – F. If there is anything else you would like to track just add additional columns.

Now just enter the information starting in row 2 such as 2/1/07, Hamburger, Lunch, etc.

Note: If you are tracking food sensitivity you can just specify if you had a reaction such as a headache or tummy ache from that particular meal. Then again if you are tracking calories then you can simply add your calories eaten each week and even average your daily calorie intake using AutoSum.

5.6.2 Timesheets

Figure 67

Create time sheets for you and your family. This will allow you to track your time used for chores and help you get an idea of time consumption. For me, I really take more breaks than anything.

You can also use it as a tool for planning out the time you will do your chores to keep everyone on schedule. Most importantly, it helps you to realize your progress even when you cannot see it from just looking around your house. Do not forget to save.

5.6.3 Medical History

Sometimes it is a great thing to know your medical history, but even more important is it to know your family's medical history. If a doctor ever asks what medications you have taken or are currently taking, you will simply print and hand-off this list. I can never remember everything when I am in the doctor's office. Open a new spreadsheet and type in Row 1 the following: **Date, Name, Medical** Condition, and **Prescription**. Now add your information starting in Row 2 accordingly.

5.6.4 Goal Setting

Do not think; document. Open to a new spreadsheet and type in Row 1 the following: **Done, Date, Goal Type, Goal, Status, Issues, Drop**. Now add information starting in Row 2 accordingly.

5.6.5 Titles Later

Figure 68

Okay. So you have some data on spreadsheets. It is time to add a formal title and maybe give you some credit for your work. Do not worry if you already have all of your information completed with calculations and all. In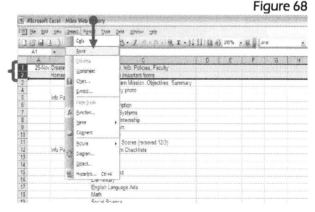
this example I created a spreadsheet that I used to outline my task checklist for a website I designed. However, this can be a great way to track anything

you work on. Then after you have completed everything on the list, it turns into a great report of your accomplishments. Pass it in to your boss just before your next review. (Hint, hint).

- Here is how to do it. You need to **Insert** two rows at the top by **selecting** Rows 1 and 2. Just move your mouse over the numbered rows while [clicking] the right mouse button.
- Now [click] the **Insert** menu and [click] Rows (hence vice versa with columns). Excel will know to add the same number of rows or columns you have selected.
- In the new A1 cell type the title of your worksheet. Do not worry if it overlaps into the other columns.

Figure 69

Microsoft Excel - Miles Web History				
File Edit View Insert Format Tools Data Window Help				
A1		*fx* Work History		100%
	A	B	C	D	E
1	Work History				
2					
3	25-Nov	Create WebPages	Created Home, Info, Policies, Faculty		
4		Homepage	Added links to important forms		
5			Inserted Program Mission, Objectives, Summary		
6			Added a faculty photo		
7		Info Page	Added Forms		

- Then increase the **Font** size to a slightly larger and bolder **Font** by **selecting** the cell in which the title resides (A1).
- [Click] the **Format** menu, then [click] **Cell**, then [click] the **Font** tab, and then [click] **Bold** / **Font Size** 16 / **Color** – **select** Red and then [click] ok.

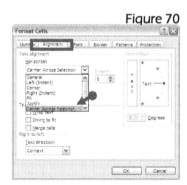

Figure 70

5.6.6 Center Across Evenly

Sometimes you want your title centered on the page above your data. You cannot just **select** the title and [click] the "Center Align" button. This only centers the data within the selected cell(s).

- Instead you need to **select** all of the columns to be included in the area you want to center the title, but only **select** them in the Row where the title is located such as ROW 1- Columns A, B, and C.

- Then [click] on the **Format** menu, **Cells**, and the **Alignment** tab.
- Next update the Horizontal section to "**Center across selection**".

Figure 71

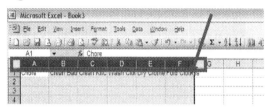

5.6.7 Resize My Columns

We have seen that a new spreadsheet's columns have a rather small width by default. This means everything we type will not fit in them precisely and that is fine. What happens when we cannot see all of the information we type? We resize of course. Resizing can be done at any time. Simply type your information into your cells and do not worry if it overlaps. Once you have your information entered then you have the option to resize all of the columns at once.

Figure 72

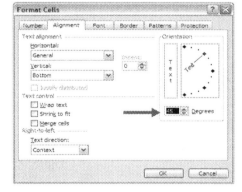

- [Click] the line between two columns and pull them apart using your left mouse button.
- Or you can **select** all of the columns (**select** the letters in the column heading using your mouse) and then double [click] one of the lines between two selected columns.

5.6.8 Angled Data

I can remember being a Brownie; not a dessert. I was a Girl Scout Brownie and a Girl Scout selling cookies. The sales form was pretty neat because the column headings were angled.

This is also a great format to use with some of your forms.

It can greatly reduce the size of the page width when you have long column names. Also it just adds a little pizzazz.

Figure 73

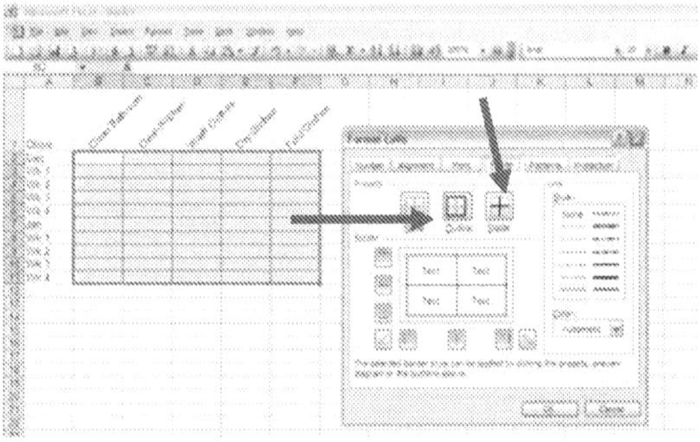

- Simply type your column names as usual.
- Then **select** the column names so we can indicate to the program which cells to apply the change to. Otherwise it does not know and so no changes are implemented.
- With the cells still selected [click] Format on the menu and **choose** Cells.
- Open the Alignment tab and change the orientation degree to **45** as shown in Figure 73.
- Press ok.
- **Select** the cells that people will be writing data into.

Figure 74

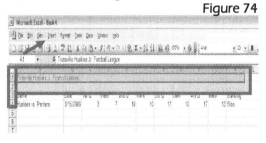

- Right [click] the selection and **choose** Format Cells.
- Open the **Border tab**.
- [Click] **Outline** and then [click] **Inside**.
- Press Ok.

5.7 Add your grids

5.7.1 Make Me Over

Let us add some formatting to our scoreboard spreadsheet started in Section 5.3.1.

- Start by inserting 2 rows for the title. Just **select** rows 1 and 2 by [clicking] on the 1 and 2 row headings on the left side of the screen.
- [Click] the **Insert** menu, then [click] **Rows**. Your two rows will be placed in the worksheet.

Figure 76

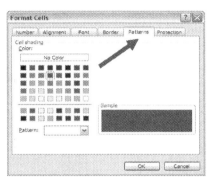

- Then type your title in A1.
- Let us dress up our title by centering it across all the data, increasing the **Font** size, and maybe changing the color. Remember we do all of this in the **Format** menu. The title has to be centered across selected cells and not <u>within</u> a cell.

Select all of the cells that will make up that space.

- Now [click] on the **Format** menu (hence changing the look) and then [click] on Cells.
- Now change the alignment by [clicking] on the **alignment tab** and changing horizontal to **center across selection**. (See Figure 77)
- Change the vertical section to **center**.
- We are not finished with formatting yet, so [click] on the **Font tab** and change the Font size to 16, **Font** style to **Bold** *Italics*, and change the

Figure 77

Font color to your league color. In this case I used green.

- [Click] ok to close.
- Now **select** your column names in row 3 and let us change that look.
- **Select** Game, Date, etc. and then [click] the **Format** menu and [click] **Cells**.
- Now [click] on the **Pattern Tab** and **select** a color for the background. Since the background will not be a white color you should change the **Font** color for better visibility.
- [Click] on the **Font tab** and **select** the color as white.
- [Click] ok.

Figure 78

- Last but not least, **select** the entire worksheet by [clicking] the ALT key and [clicking] the A key simultaneously.
- [Click] on the **Format** menu and [click] **Rows** then **Height**.

- Enter the number "20" into the height area. Feel free to highlight some of your cells and add the gridlines.

Figure 79

- I also changed the font color of each game I added in. The first is in black, the next in blue, the next in red, etc.

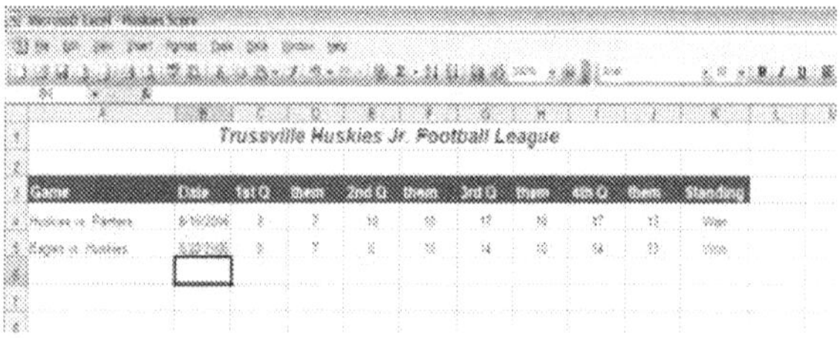

Figure 80

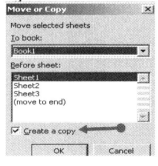

5.7.2 Clone My Worksheet

Sometimes you have a perfect spreadsheet and you want to use it time and time again while preserving the original such as a monthly budget. Why overwrite the July budget with August when you can create another one in a matter of seconds? Clone it.

- Simply [click] the **Edit** menu and **Move or Copy Sheet**.

- For **Book choose** the current name of this workbook. However, you can **choose** new book if you want a new separate spreadsheet to be saved under another name.
- Also **choose** a **Before sheet**, which in this case I will select **Sheet1**. Lastly, check the **Create a copy** button to clone otherwise you will just move the same sheet around.
- [Click] ok.

Note: I used this tool in the office the following ways:

Co-workers wanted a copy of a specific spreadsheet and I did not want them to have the entire workbook. I copied the spreadsheet they needed to a new book and just sent that new book to them.

I sometimes create very complex spreadsheets where I do not want to ruin hours of work. So at each important milestone I create copies within the workbook and name the sheets as Drafts in sequential order. Draft 1, Draft 2, etc. This is a way to save different versions. After some significant progress I copy that sheet as Ver1, Ver2, etc. So if I ever make an unfixable mistake I can simply go to the previous copy and would not have to scrap everything.

5.7.3 AutoFormat Me

Sometimes it is time consuming to get a specific look for your spreadsheet. Good news, there is an Autoformat feature that allows you to choose a look and apply the attributes that you like. Open your completed allowance schedule or any other spreadsheet you would like to try to auto format.

Figure 81

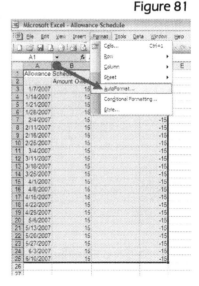

- **Select** all your content information that should be formatted.
- [Click] the **Format** menu and [click] **AutoFormat**.

- **Select** the style of formatting you would like your spreadsheet to mirror such as Classic 2 or Accounting 2 and then [click] the

Figure 82

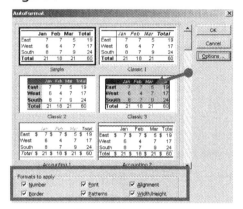

Options button located on the right side of the dialog box.

- All of the options are at the bottom with checkboxes. Uncheck any of the options you do not want applied to you data.

- I am leaving all of mine checked at this time, but if I did not like the Font I could simply uncheck and retain the font I created in my spreadsheet originally.

- [Click] the ok button and your spreadsheet will look just like the chosen design.

- If you do not like the chosen design just repeat until you find one that you like.

- I have also used this feature numerous times on the job because it is a quick and easy method to add a nice design to my spreadsheets.

Figure 83

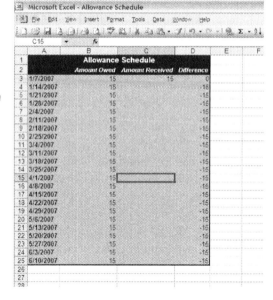

6 Point Me To The Power

6.1 Games

Figure 84

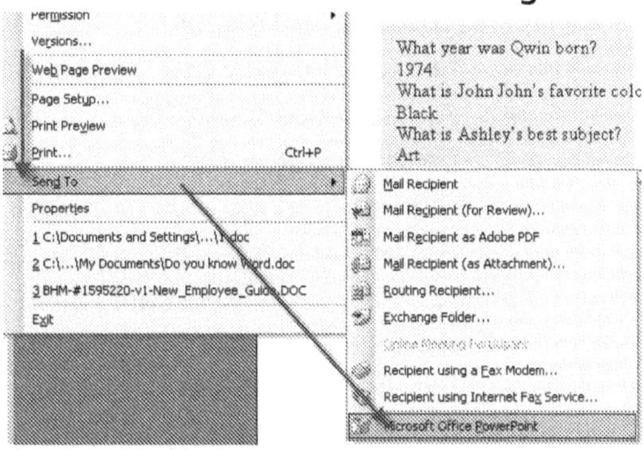

6.1.1 Beat The Clock

Create an activity that requires a quick answer response. In this example I use a fun activity that can be used with friends or family in a light hearted manner. The questions can range from "very general" to "very personal" depending on who will try to beat the clock. I am going to show you a very easy way to quickly create your slideshow after you have compiled your questions in Microsoft Word®. This will also make it easier for the whole family to collaborate if you create a Beat the Clock as a holiday or family activity. Can you not see all of the siblings trying to beat the clock? Best of all, people get a chance to learn something in a fun activity.

- In Microsoft Word, type a question.
- Press enter to go to a new line.
- Type the answer to that question.
- Press enter and type the next question and so on until all questions are in the document. I have a total of four for this example. If you'd rather work from PowerPoint then click the outline tab and type your questions and answers in that view.

Figure 85

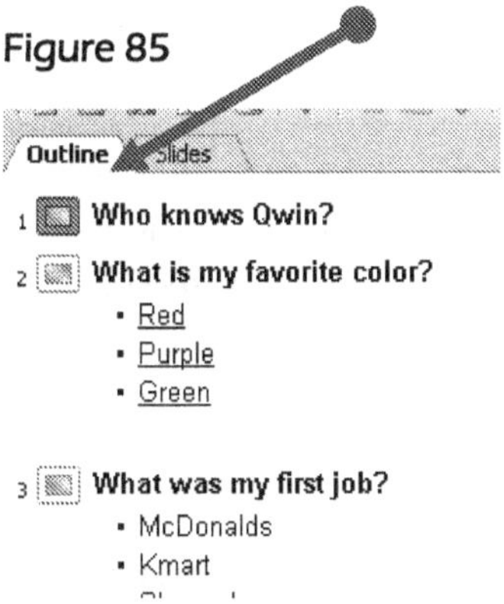

- [Click] **File** on the menu and **select** Send To . (For Word users only).
- Then **choose** Microsoft PowerPoint.

- When Microsoft PowerPoint® opens, [click] the Outline tab (see Figure 85) so you can work directly with the text rather than with the slides. As you structure the text it will automatically update the slides.
- Depending on your setup, you will have to **promote** (paragraph becomes the title of the slide) or **demote** (becomes a bulleted item on the previous slide) some of the text.
- All questions should be promoted to the highest level by pressing **Shift + Tab**. Refer to the questions that have a square slide icon/image next to them in Figure 85. The paragraph will not promote if it is already at the highest level.
- Now if your answers are not in a bulleted format then perform the following check-action:
- Check: Is the answer at the 1st level; the title for a slide? (The paragraph would be bolded with the slide icon on the same line.)
  - Press **Enter** to separate the answers from the question onto their own lines.
  - Then [click] your cursor in the paragraph to be demoted, press **Tab** to demote it to a bullet.

You may have to practice to get the hang of it.

Note: You may leave the outline pane by [clicking] the **Slide tab** (next to the outline tab we clicked earlier). Then you can just type your questions and answers directly on the slide as a work around until you can practice and get the hang of promoting and demoting text.

- After all of the text is in the proper position, press **Edit** from the menu and **Select All**. Notice all of the slides have blue outlines indicating they are selected.

Figure 86

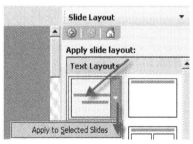

- With the slides still selected, [click] **Format** from the menu and **Slide Layout**. All of the available layouts will load in the Task Pane located on the right side of the screen.
- **Choose** the very first layout which is Title Slide (this would be similar to a title page).
- [Click] the arrow of the Title Slide layout and **choose** "Apply to Selected Slides".

- Now that we've done the task of choosing a *layout*, we need to go on to the next task of choosing a nice *design*.
- [Click] the Task Pane down arrow next to words **Slide Layout**.
- Change the task from **Slide Layout** to **Slide Design**.

Figure 87

- Now **choose** one of the designs that load in the Task Pane by [clicking] the arrow next to the design and **selecting** Apply to All Slides.
- We are not done just yet. Now while all of the slides are still selected (if yours do not have a blue outline border then just go back to **Edit** on the menu and **choose** Select All), change the task from **Slide Design** to **Slide Animation Schemes**.
- Simply [click] on a couple of different animation schemes to find one you like. I used Elegant in the Slideshow I created.
- We are almost done. Change the task from **Slide Design** to **Slide Transition** (how our slides will move one to the other).
- **Choose** a transition effect that you like. You can change the speed if that is an option. I have chosen Fast and have also added a Drum Roll sound. All your slides can have different effects if you **select** them one at a time. Or you can **select** several by holding down the Ctrl key and [clicking] all of the slides in which you would like to apply the design.
- Now we will go to the Advance slide section of the task pane (you must be in the **Slide Transition** task to see this), then uncheck "On mouse click" and check "Automatically after".

Figure 88

- Then insert a time such as 20 seconds as shown in Figure 88.
- Now you are ready to play the game.
- [Click] **Slideshow** from the menu and **select** **View Show** (or simply [click] **F5** on your keyboard).

6.1.2 Timers

Countdown Timers are available on www.office.microsoft.com already designed and working.

Figure 89

- Simply [click] on templates. Type the word "timer" into the search box and [click] search and download the one you like.

- I use them as a countdown in class. "We will resume in 10 minutes". They also can be use with your kids on time out or just to time a task such as having 15 minutes to straighten up their rooms. Your kids will learn to use them on their own and time themselves while doing homework, on punishment, etc.

6.1.3 Trivia Game

"Multiple choice" is the name of the game. This can be a Thanksgiving family gathering activity about "Let us see who knows the most about movies" to a special "How well do my honey and children know me"?

- Simply create a question as the title for each slide. Let us just do 10 questions for the first time. That means we will have a cover slide at the beginning where the title is the name of the game. Add any subtitle you would like.
- Now insert a new slide by [clicking] the **Insert** button on the menu.
- [Click] **New Slide**.
- [Click] the title placeholder located at the top of the slide – it says "Click here to insert title".
- Type the first question for the trivia game. My question is "What is my favorite color?"
- Now [click] where it says to "Click to add text".

- Then list 2 or 3 answer choices in the bulleted list, yet for this slide only make sure the correct answer is the first choice at least until you learn to link them.
- [Click] in a blank area of the slide to deselect a placeholder.
- Now build the other 10 questions slides by [clicking] **Insert** on the menu and <u>selecting</u> **New Slide**.
- Repeat the previous 4 steps until you are done with all of your questions and answers.

Note: You will have to hyperlink all of the answers so that when

Figure 90

they are [clicked] they will route the user to another location. The correct answer choice should be linked to advance to the "Next slide". The next slide will be the next question or the final congratulations slide. However, all of the wrong answers should all advance to a hidden slide that indicates the user has chosen the wrong answer. This means you should create the wrong answer slide prior to setting up your links.

- Insert a **New Slide**. Notice that the New Slide inserts just after the currently <u>selected</u> slide.

- Type a title for the New Slide – "Wrong Answer" or something to that effect.
- Then in the "Add text" textbox simply type a message letting the user know they have to start over by [clicking] the button on the slide.

Figure 91

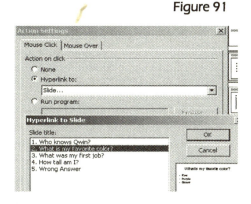

- Now [click] **Slideshow** from the menu and <u>select</u> **Action Buttons**.
- You can <u>choose</u> any of the buttons, but I have chosen the return button that looks like a "U'" with an arrow.
- Use your mouse to draw your button onto the slide. Simply [click], drag, and then release.

73

- The action button window opens automatically. Setup the action as follows: Hyperlink = slide = slide 2 (your 1st question).
- Now let us go and setup all of the answers on the slides to link to the appropriate places. All of the wrong answers will link to the wrong answer slide you have just created.
- In the slides thumbnail pane on the left [click] on the 2nd slide.
- **Select**/Highlight the first answer choice.
- Right [click] the selection to open a shortcut menu.

Figure 92

- [Click] **Hyperlink**.
- We are only creating a link for this one bulleted item. The hyperlink window opens.
- [Click] the second option "Place in this document" located in the "Link to" area on the left slide.
- Then **choose** slide option named "Next

Figure 93

Slide" located towards the center.

- [Click] ok.
- Now **select**/highlight the next answer choice to be hyperlinked.
- Right [click] the selection and **choose** Hyperlink.

- Instead of linking to the next slide, this answer should be linked to the Wrong Answer slide. So find the wrong answer slide in the list of slides and double [click] it.
- Repeat for the other answer(s).
- If you make a mistake with the hyperlink, simply right [click] the answer and **choose** "**Edit hyperlink**".
- Repeat for all of the question slides.

- Once all answers have been hyperlinked, [click] **Slideshow** from the menu and <u>choose</u> "**Slide Transition**".

Figure 94

- On the right side of the screen you will notice your task pane lists different options for the way your slide will appear in and disappear out; hence transition between one another.
- <u>**Choose**</u> an option such as Newsflash.
- Then uncheck the mouse click option in the Advance slide section.
- [Click] "Apply to All Slides".
- We are about to wrap it up, but how about adding a nice background to the Slideshow? [Click] **Format** on the menu and <u>**choose**</u> **Slide Design**.
- Find the design you like in the task pane located on the right side of your screen and just [click] it.
- Your activity is ready to test out. Simple press your F5 key on your keyboard.

6.2 Homework

Figure 95

6.2.1 Spelling Practice

This one uses the narration feature of PowerPoint. Create the cover slide where the title is something like "Week 2 Spelling".

First we want to **choose** our **Slide Design** (The look/format).

- [Click] **Format** on the menu and **choose** **Slide Design**.
- Now [click] "Click to add title" to add your title.
- [Click] to add a subtitle which should be something to the effect of narrated by John.
- Now [click] **Insert** on the menu and **select** **New Slide**.
- [Click] where it says click to add a title and type "Spell".
- Then [click] in the add text section and type the first spelling word. I am using the word "Important".

Now we have to add our animation to the slide. What we want is to _see_ the word Spell and then _hear_ the narrated spelling word to be spelled. Then in 10 seconds we want the correct spelling of the word to appear giving your child enough time to recite or write down the word just before checking it. When they are ready for the next word, we want them to simply [click] the mouse to see spell and hear the next word. Let us setup the animation first, then we will come back and add the narration.

Figure 96

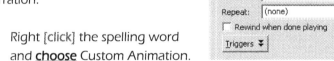

- Right [click] the spelling word and **choose** Custom Animation.
- Then in the task pane [click] the **Add Effect** button and **choose** entrance.
- **Choose** More effects.

- **Choose** "Spinner" under the Moderate section.
- Now we need to program exactly when and how the animation will appear. [Click] the drop down arrow next to the listed animation and **choose Timing**.
- When the effect window opens, make sure you [click] on the **Timing** tab.

Figure 97

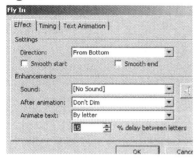

- **Choose** to start "After Previous".
- **Choose** to delay 7-10 seconds.
- **Choose** a medium speed.
- Now [click] the "Effects" tab.
- Change the animate text to "By letter"
- Change the % delay to 20.
- Press ok.

Do not worry if the 7 second delay is adequate at this time. When the narration is added, it will change anyway.

Let us create the other spelling words. Since we want them all to work in the same exact manner, we will insert a duplicate slide rather than a new one. This will create a clone with all of the animations intact.

- [Click] **Insert** on the menu and **choose Duplicate slide**.
- Repeat for the number of spelling words you will add to the Slideshow.
- Now [click] slide 3 which should be the 2nd spelling word slide. **Select** and delete the bulleted word (Information in my case) and type the new word (Territory). Your kids can actually take over at this point.
- Repeat for all of the rest of the words, but keep a list of the exact order. You will have to narrate the words and will not be able to see them on the slides.
- Do not forget to save your work throughout with all of my activities.
- Now with all of the spelling words on different slides, let us add the voice.

You must have a microphone and sound devices setup on your computer to create the voice part. You can test it in the Microsoft PowerPoint® application as described next.

- [Click]Slideshow on the menu and **choose** Record Narration.
- The Record Narration window opens. [Click] the **Set Microphone Level** button. However, your sound must already be installed and working.
- You can also see that the maximum number of minutes to record is displayed.
- You have a checkbox to link the narration file rather than make it part of the presentation itself, but the spelling words will not create too big of a file so we do not have to use that option.

Figure 98

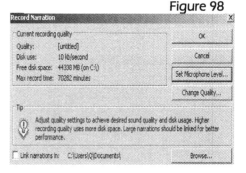

- When you are ready to record simply [click] ok. I let my children record their own spelling words and they seem to like it. My son also phrases it in a sentence.
- Warning: as you record, you will [click] through the Slideshow. Say the word directly after the title "Spell" appears and before you [click] to reveal the spelling word. You may have to practice several times to get the timing. Therefore, the order is as follows:
- [Click] to show the spelling word slide and you will see the word Spell.
- Then say the word.
- Then count to yourself 7 seconds.
- Then [click] the mouse to reveal the word.
- Now [click] the mouse to go to the next slide that will show the word Spell.
- Say that word and count to yourself for 7 seconds.
- Then [click] to reveal the word.
- Keep repeating those steps until you get to the end.

At the very end you will be shown a time length for the entire presentation and be asked to keep or discard the narration. **Choose** "keep" because you can always redo any of the slides individually by **selecting** that slide and starting the **Record Narration** from that point. If you have younger children you can just pass the slideshow down for later when they get in that grade.

6.2.2 Book Report

Figure 99

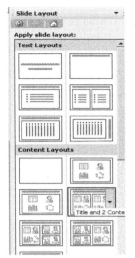

This exercise also uses the narration feature, but you will have to be careful when recording a large media file. It works best with small stories or books broken into chapters. I recommend no more than several small chapters per slideshow. After my children have read a book that they really like, they go online to find pictures of the book cover, items referenced in the book, etc. So if the book talks about green eggs and ham, they find pictures or clipart of green eggs, eggs in general, and ham. One resource is Google – Images.

- Start a new presentation from **File** on the menu and **select** New.
- Then create a title – the book title will do.
- Add a subtitle – narrated by Ashley.
- Now add a New Slide by [clicking] **Insert** on the Menu and **selecting** New Slide.
- Add 5 – 10 more new slides because this show will consist strictly of images and a narrator's voice.
- Now let us change the layout of the 2nd slide. We have worked with a bulleted list thus far, but now we have images we would like to add.
- [Click] **Format** on the menu because the layout deals with the look of the slide and **choose** Slide Layout.
- Now in the task pane **choose** from the **Content Layout** section; "Title and 2 content". As you hover over each, a name appears naming that particular layout.

Figure 100

Insert Clip Art

icon to ac

- We will hold off on a adding the title at this point, but let us add an image of some eggs.
- From the slide itself, simply [click] the icon

:ontent

that represents the type of image you would like to add.
- In this case I have [clicked] the clipart icon – the last one on row one that looks like a cartoon figure.
- However if you have a picture on your computer you would like to use, **choose** the picture icon – the 1st one on the second row that looks like a mountain. Find your picture and **double** [click] it.

Figure 101

- Yet, if you [click] the clipart icon you will open the search window.
- Simply type in a word such as eggs and [click] search.
- After the images load simply [click] the one you are interested in and it will be resized to fit your content placeholder on the Slideshow.
- Repeat for the content placeholder on the other side of your slide. I will search for ham this time.
- Notice when you actually look at your slide thumbnail you cannot see the words "Click here to add a title". That only appears while you are in edit mode for instructional purposes.
- Change the layout of the other slides as you would like. Try out a couple of different ones.
- However, if you want several or all of your slides to have the same layout, just hold down the Ctrl key and [click] the different slide thumbnails in the slide pane. This will allow you to apply the layout to all selected slides simultaneously.

6.2.3 Books On ~~Tape~~ PowerPoint

Figure 102

Create this one in the same way as the book report in Section 6.2.2. However, let your child actual read a short book or a few chapters of a book. Then burn a copy of it and send to the grandparents. My mom was very surprised to hear and see her grandchildren reading on an animated CD presentation. They can create a whole series. If you have a projector, make a big deal of it and your kids will love to read. I would not suggest typing all of the words of the story because it will take away when people listen to it. However, interesting pictures and animation will add to the show.

6.2.4 Quiz Me

My family and my students love this one. They just think it is so funny and entertaining, but they learn something at the same time. Gather some questions like in the Beat the Clock activity. However, this one should have two or more answer choices on the same slide to choose from. It is more of a multiple choice/ true-false type of game. Then create 10 or so slides with the question in the title area and the answers in the text area. At the end of the Slide Show create a slide that says something to the effect of "Wrong answer". This slide will automatically return them to the previously viewed slide. I also used it

Figure 103

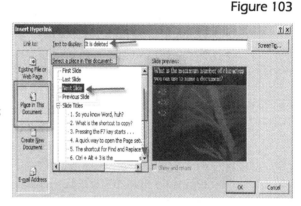

for myself when studying for my Real Estate broker's exam and passed. This is how to set it up.

Create all of your slides first. I usually type my questions in Microsoft Word® and send them to Microsoft PowerPoint®. Then **select** each answer choice one by one. With the answer choice **selected**, right [click] on it and **choose** Hyperlink.

6.2.5 Progression Slideshow

Figure 104

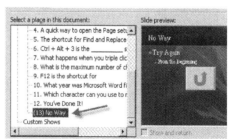

This is a great idea to use for a wedding reception, baby shower, anniversary, birthday party, memorial, family reunion, high school reunion, or any special occasion. The idea is to have pictures appear in and out automatically that reflect the life of an individual, couple, or group. The hardest part is gathering the pictures you will include in the slideshow, but once you have them scanned or saved from a digital camera you are half way there.

- First, make sure you know where your pictures are located on your computer. Are they all in the "My pictures" folder or somewhere else? It does not matter, but it would be quicker if they all were in the same place, preferably one folder.
- Open Microsoft PowerPoint®.
- The program opens to a single blank cover slide. Simply [click] and type your title in the textbox that states "Click here to add title". I would say something to the effect of "xxyears Together. Then [click] to add your subtitle just below it. "Happy Anniversary John and Qwin". (Can you not see the kids starting a side business/hobby creating beautiful Slide Shows)?
- Before we go any further let us **choose** a slide design. Just [click] **Format** on the menu and **choose** **Slide Design**. You may not have any templates that will fit your occasion so you will have to go to the Microsoft.com® website

Figure 106

Microsoft Office Online

* Connect to Microsoft Office Online

Web Page on Microsoft Office Online
PowerPoint

and download one. Just press your F1 key on your keyboard for help.

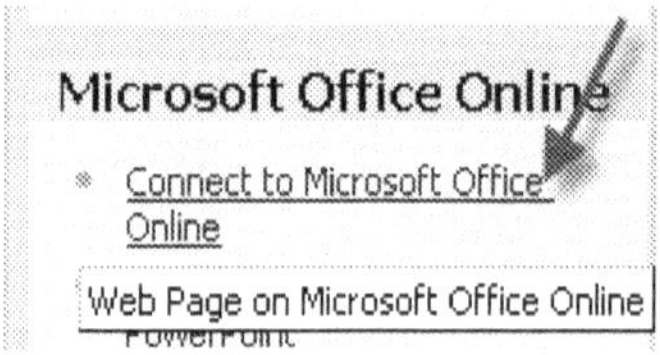

Figure 105

- Then [click] the "Connect to Microsoft Office Online" option and search for templates.
- Once on the website, [click] Templates as shown in Figure 107.
- Then search for an abstract presentation as shown in Figure 105.

- When the templates load pay close attention to the version because your software may be too

Figure 107

outdated to run that template. Although I can use anything

with a version of PowerPoint 2003 or older, I cannot use PowerPoint 2007.

Figure 108

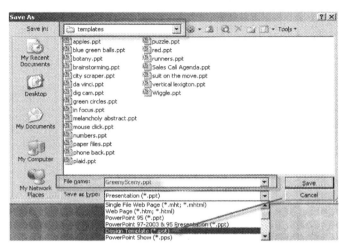

I am too cheap to get the new stuff, but I am sure I will budge sooner or later. Mothers must use what we have so that we can at least afford a pedicure every once in a while.

- If you do not see any that you like, just perform another search, but try to include the word "presentation" so that you do not have to scroll through so many. You only want to see presentations after all.

Figure 109

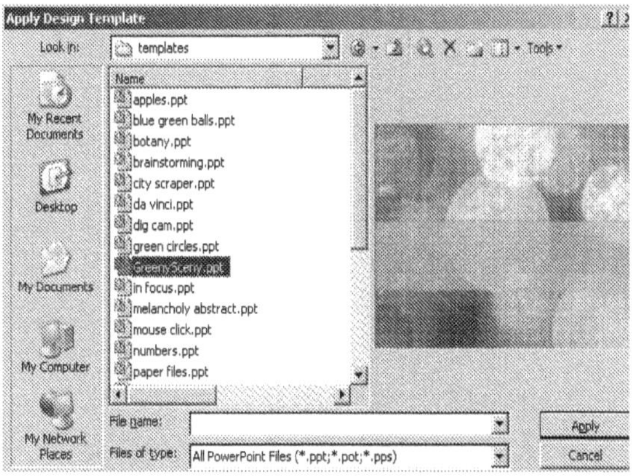

- Download as instructed by the website.
- Once the presentation opens on your computer, you need to save it as a template to use later. [Click] **File** on the menu and **choose** Save As. Or you can press your F12 key on your keyboard.
- Then **choose** the Save in location folder so you will be able to find it later.
- Create a file name for it. I just made up something I will remember later – GreenySceny.

83

Figure 110

Browse...

- Then **choose** a **file type**: Design Template. There many types for presentations. The default is Presentation **.ppt** which you may use later.

6.3 Training

6.3.1 Multimedia Checklist/Rules

Create instructional slides that presenting how things should be done from A - Z. If you have a special procedure for taking out the trash, put it in this format and on paper. Something more helpful may be the Rules of house that your kids should go over with their visiting friends. On the last slide, put some type of confirmation such as if you understand these rules come tell John's mom rule #2 to get a SURPRISE!

6.3.2 Cleaning Duty

If you cannot keep up with paper, then creating a series of "How to clean" presentations may be a viable option. Make is funny though. You can insert videos into your presentation as well as pictures using the content layouts. Just keep them short. As a first trial, create training about how to clean the bathroom and let your children guest star in the photos. Show dad washing the dishes or you putting your hair into a ponytail. Add pictures as you go along. Make sure when using steps, create a title that coordinates with each step. So slide 2 will be Step 1 because slide 1 will be the title/cover slide.

6.3.3 Make-up/Shaving Tips/Tying a Tie

You do not have to be a cosmetologist to do this one, but it does not hurt. Ladies; when you find time have your daughter or niece take pictures of you while applying your makeup. Gentlemen; Have your son or nephew take pictures of you the next time your shave. Or if you prefer, have your honey take the pictures and get the family involved in creating the show. Then setup a show that breaks down the steps into easy to follow directions. The layout should be Title, Text, and Content so that you can bullet the steps and include a picture all on one slide.

6.4 Family Entertainment

6.4.1 Photo Gallery

The photo gallery can be any group of pictures you would like to have displayed automatically. They can be pictures from a vacation, school trip, a history of photos from baby to teen years, etc. Instead of someone turning the pages of a photo album, it will be done through automation on the computer. So instead of sending the relatives a duplicate copy of a few photos just send them a whole album or couple of albums where you narrate what is going on in some of the shots. It makes a nice holiday gift especially for long distance relatives. Just have all of the members of the family get together as a family activity and record a freestyle discussion of the photos as they appear.

Figure 111

- Open a new Presentation.
- Type a title for this photo gallery such as "The Humphries Family".
- Type a subtitle such as "In Miami".
- **Select** a design by [clicking] **Format** on the menu and **choosing Slide Design**.
- From the task pane [click] the design you like best. If you decide on another just [click] it.
- While we are here, let us add an animation scheme that will provide consistent movement throughout the slides. Simply [click] the drop arrow of the task pane located towards to top right and beside the word **Slide Design.**
- [Click] the **Slide Design – Animation Schemes** option from the list.
- The schemes are listed by category so scroll down to the exciting and try Float. Just [click] it.

- If that does not work out for you then scroll through and [click] some until you find one you like. Make sure your auto preview is checked (at the very bottom right of the screen).
- Once that is done let us insert some new slides to add our pictures. Just press the Ctrl key and hold on your keyboard and press the letter "M" on the keyboard about 20 more times. Release all keys.
- **Select** the last slide in the slide pane then scroll up until you can see slide 2. Now hold down the shift key and [click] slide 2. All slides in between will be selected. If you have any trouble, try it a couple of times. Just make sure you [click] the last one and hold down shift and then [click] the first one (or vice versa).
- Right [click] any selected slide and **choose** **Slide Layout**, which opens in the task pane.
- Look down in the category of Content Layouts and **choose** the "Title, and 2 Content" option (2nd one on row 2). Remember to hover so you can see the names. This layout is applied to all selected slides.
- I am used this layout so I can give a title, but feel free to use any layout you want that has a content placeholder.
- Now [click] slide 2 in the slide pane so only that one is selected.
- [Click] the picture icon to browse for your photos. Dbl–[click] the picture you would like to insert.
- Do the same for the other content placeholder. The picture will auto resize as necessary to fit in the placeholder. However, you can resize it manually by **selecting** the picture (one [click]) and dragging one of the 6 handles that look like round white circles. Just [click] and drag in or out to resize.
- Repeat until you have all of your photos arranged to your liking.
- You may rearrange your slides simply by [clicking] and holding the slide thumbnail in the slide pane and dragging and dropping to the desired location.
- Use the **Record Narration** feature under the **Slide Show** menu as described in the Spelling Practice presentation. See Section 6.2.1 for instructions.

6.4.2   Family Reunion Fun

Take some of your past family reunion pictures and scan or save them to one file. This will make it easier when browsing. I would say use about 50 or so photos if possible. Get the family together and pick out the family favorites, individual favorites, and of course the worse of the worse. After all, American Idol has proven that people love to see the worse of the bunch. Create an album, but use a layout that includes text so that you can list the names of the people in the photos. Remember to name them from left to right.

If you really want a challenge, try creating the slides with links that when clicked send the user to a relative of the person.

Figure 112

Baby Pictures

- You can add text that says "Click the photo to see John's mother and father".
- To hyperlink photos simply right [click] the photo and **choose** Action Settings. This is just an alternative to **choosing** Hyperlink, but feel free to use the hyperlink feature.
- Then from the "**Mouse click**" tab, **select** "Hyperlink to".
- [Click] the drop arrow and **choose** "Slide".
- Find the slide that has the picture of the relative you would like the link to.
- Press ok.
- Now open the slide that the photo was linked to and add an action button that returns the viewer to the last viewed slide. Simply [click] **Slide Show** on the menu and **choose Action buttons**.
- **Choose** the return button that looks like the "U" with an arrow.
- Then drag and draw out the return button onto the side.
- It should default to hyperlink to the "**Last Slide Viewed**". If not just **select** that option.

Now when the viewer clicks to see John's parents they can [click] the return button to return to John's slide and continue the show.

6.4.3   About My Family

This can be a progressive "family through the years" type of thing. Let your kids share memories and narrate some of the great things about the family. Examples could be mom and dad got married. Then create a slide with a picture of the family of three. Then create another addition showing the family grew to four. Then create the family of five. I am afraid to keep going.

7 Are you still out looking?

Figure 113

Microsoft Outlook® will help you and your family to stay on track and possibly help bridge communication gaps. This program is a great organizational management system. Additionally it is where you can store information about your friends, family, and acquaintances. It also has a place for you to keep a journal and notes. The best part about this one for me is that is syncs (sends data between) my cell phone so all of my appointments and contacts go wherever I go. Although you can check your emails using Microsoft Outlook®, it is not an email provider. You must have an email account setup with a provider first such as hotmail, yahoo, AOL, your cable or phone company, etc. If you already have an email account, check with your provider on the setup instructions for using Microsoft Outlook® with your account or simply incorporate my ideas using your web based email instead. You certainly may use the other tools such as the calendar, tasks and journal without utilizing the email. I also use this program for my school email when teaching. When my students submit their lesson, they are automatically organized and categorized in a special manner. Then I have a few other email accounts setup in my Outlook folder as well.

I do not know about you, but I have so many things going on in a day that I just cannot remember them all. I am not good a writing things down and keeping up with notes either. One thing I know for sure is that I will look at my computer everyday or even better have my cell phone with me. I usually keep only my personal items on my home computer and work on the work computer. The best thing is that what I have mastered at home, I implement at work to stay on top of the job. Practice, Practice, Practice is great, but implementation is the true test from which we learn.

7.1 Email

7.1.1 Tell Me; I Tell You

All during the week while I am not at the store I get requests for things I need to pick up on my next trip to the store. Okay – when that trip comes, which may be spontaneous, I usually do not have the several lists of the items my family has put together. So I had to implement another system. Encourage your children to email you items they want from the grocery store, things they would like to do this weekend, dates they want to sleepover with friends, etc.

Then you respond to them via email. They will get an edge on typing and emailing. An example is when my daughter runs out of pencils and my son needs paper, they send me an email. In the beginning I had to keep reminding

Figure 114

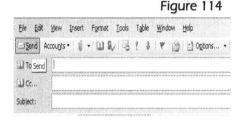

them to email me, but they got use to it. Then I would check my email or they would let me know they sent me a message. I would drag that email message to my calendar and setup an appointment to get them their supplies. Now the list is actually sitting in my calendar for that date I chose on the calendar. I would send them a message back to let them know I am on it. It was great because it encourages them to place thought behind their requests and structure them into sentences. Also you all will practice checking your sent folders to see any past messages sent out that may need to be followed up.

- [Click] the **New** button to create a message. If using another email source like your internet email you most likely will need to [click] **Compose**.
- In the To: field, enter the email address of the recipient(s). In the CC: field; enter anyone else who should get a copy of this email. This can include your email address if you would like.
- If there is more than one recipient, simply separate them with a semi-colon.
- Type the message in the large white textbox.
- Remember to press the **Send** button.

7.1.2 ePal

Hook your kids up with Grandma, a cousin, or a sibling who is also learning to use a computer for email and Internet purposes. They can partner together to improve on communicating via email while keeping in touch. You would be surprise how two 10 year olds can stay abreast of one another. Another alternative is for them to ePal their friends at school or just with you. It may be best to set a day of the week to check messages. Some people are not married to the computer like I am. So something like check emails every Wednesday may be a good thing to decide on before hand. Another consideration is to set aside a block time for creating and responding to emails. Having a discussion via email takes time just as a phone conversation does. Dedicate 6-6:30 to ePal-ing. Just remember to go the **View** menu and **Refresh** your screen. Once they have the hang of it, add a few more pals in to make it a group thing.

7.1.3 When You Tell Me Then Tell Dad Too

To:, CC:, BCC:. To: is the intended recipient(s). CC: is a person that should get a copy. BCC: is a blind copy where the person that should get a copy actually receives a copy in secret. While anyone who receives the message can view the To: and the CC:, they cannot view the BCC:. BCC is probably the most beneficial at work. The way to use this in the family is to have your children send their messages to you and CC: dad so he will know that they have communicated with you. So if Ashley

Figure 115

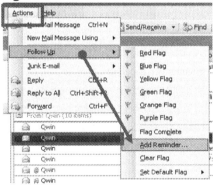

asks for $20 for a field trip due by Friday dad will be notified and may cough up the money 1st.By the way I usually place the email into my calendar to remind me that she is going somewhere so I can have snacks, clothes, etc. ready before the trip.

7.1.4 Follow Up (Color Flags)

Sometimes you receive an email while you are very busy, but you know for certain you can take care of it shortly. Or you get an email that you need to return a call to the person tomorrow to get further details. Or you want the email reminder redelivered to you at another time so that it will be fresh on your mind. Yet, you do not want to clutter your calendar or tasks. Use

Figure 116

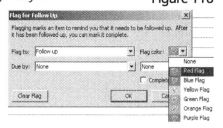

your follow up flags to help. Different color flags are available to help you coordinate your follow ups. Your kids can also use this to help remind them of things. It is fast and easy.

- First, **select** an email that you need to follow up on later.

Figure 117

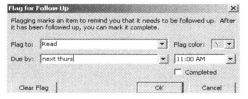

- [Click] **Actions** on the menu.
- [Click] **Follow-up**.
- [Click] **Add Reminder**.
- Setup your flag. As shown in Figure 116 you can change the

Flag to: Call, FYI, Reply, Review, Read, etc. In this case I will use READ.

- **Choose** a flag color that means something to you.
- [Click] on the **Due by**: arrow to open the calendar.
- Note: In Microsoft Outlook®, you can simply type references to dates such as "Next Thurs", "today", "2 months before", or "2nd Sat" and it will automatically insert that corresponding date. See Figure 117 and try it out!
- **Choose** a time and [click] ok.

- The email in your inbox now has a colored flag and the follow up is posted to a special "Follow up" folder.

Figure 118

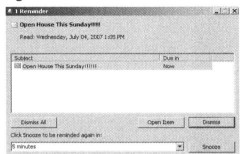

- When the reminder date and time arrives, a pop-up window opens to alert you of the follow up as shown in Figure 118. You can open the item to see the details of the email, snooze for up to 2 weeks, or dismiss the reminder all together. I use the snooze all of the time because I am sometimes busy when the reminder appears. It is great because I choose to be reminded in an hour or tomorrow.

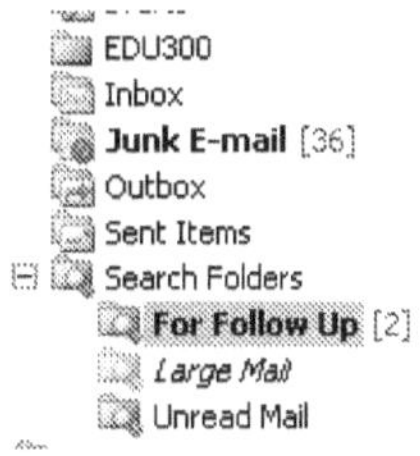

- Since the follow up does not appear in your calendar, there is a special folder that all follow up messages default to called "For Follow Up".

Figure 119

- The For Follow Up folder can be opened simply by [clicking] the **Expand** button for **Search Folders** on the left side of the screen if not already expanded.

- Then [click] **For Follow Up**.
- Also, the message in your inbox turns red after the due date.

Figure 120

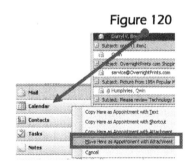

7.1.5 Move Me Where I Need To Be

Some messages are informative, some are entertaining, others may relate to a meeting or task.

- To setup an appointment regarding an email you receive, simply **select** that message.

- Right [click] and drag the message onto the **calendar icon** or button as shown in Figure 120.

Figure 121

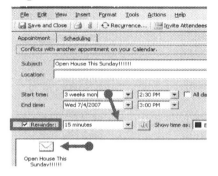

- By right [clicking] and dragging you are presented with options to either copy or move the message into a new appointment. I like to move because it lets me clean out my inbox at the same time. However, I would have perform and advanced search to find the email again. So there are pros and cons.

- Now you must setup your appointment date and time. You can use the calendar by [clicking] the **Start Date** field or use the user friendly phrases as shown earlier such as "2 weeks". I have typed in the Start date: "3 weeks mon" and pressed enter for my example. It automatically sets the date to the 3rd Monday from the current date.

- Note: Be careful because typing "3rd Mon" will prompt the 3rd Monday of the current month. I actually wanted 3 Mondays away from the date I was setting it up.

- Change the **End time**. The appointment can last for several days or months if you would like. For example, when I go on vacation at work I would add an appointment from that Monday that ends on that Friday.

- The next important thing is to setup a reminder if this is

Figure 122

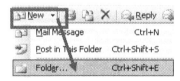

something you must prepare for or should be reminded about in advance. It works like a charm and has saved me from missing more events than I can count.

- **Save** and **Close** the appointment when done. *[File menu]*.

- [Click] on your **Calendar** icon or button to view your calendar.
- [Click] the **Date** in which you set the appointment and you will see it right there on the calendar.

- If you would like to setup a task rather than appointment, simply right [click] and drag to the **task icon** and execute the same steps.

7.1.6 Drag And Drop Your Emails Into Organized Folders

To get even more organized, set up folders as though your inbox was a file drawer. We get so many emails these days that we often need to file them away for safekeeping. I have folders in my work email as well as in my personal email. Let us set up a couple of folders: Job, School, Personal, Others.

Figure 123

- **Select** the arrow on the **New** button.
- [Click] **Folder**.
- Then type a name for the new folder such as Family.
- **Select** the folder type in the Folder contain drop box. Just **select Mail and Post Items** as shown in Figure 123. However, you can create other things such as additional calendars for each family member with their name for the calendar names. This is an option if you share a computer.
- Now **choose** the location where the new folder will reside. Let us **choose** Inbox. This means it will be created within your inbox. However, you can **select** Personal Folders and it will create at the same level as your Inbox folder. Just expand the Inbox folder in not already expanded and **select** the folder named Family.

Figure 124

- As you receive messages about family issues save them to the new Family folder by dragging them there.

7.1.7 Folders (Lock 'em Up)

If you have just one computer or a community shared computer, you still can achieve some privacy with your folders. All you have to do is create a password for your Personal Folders folder. The items in that folder cannot be viewed without entering the correct password.

Figure 125

- Right [click] your Personal Folders folder as shown in Figure 125.
- **Select** Properties.
- [Click] Advanced.
- [Click] Password.
- Add your password. Note: You will also come here to change the password.

7.1.8 Group Distribution

No need to send emails to one person at a time. Also, there is no need to try to remember the email addresses of the list of people you normally include on emails. If you are doing this activity one with your children they should start with creating a group of the immediate family members' email addresses. These are people they will email when they have made the honor roll or won the soccer game.

Figure 126

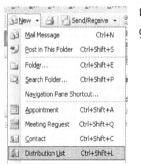

- [Click] the drop down arrow on the **New** button.
- **Select Distribution List**.
- If you have the addresses already setup in your Outlook contact then [click] the **Select Members** button and

just [click] to add each person that should be added. Otherwise you will need to setup each person now.

- [Click] the **Add New** button and fill in the details as requested to setup a person's email address.

Figure 127

- As a side note I would suggest setting up the emails in your Contacts first because you will have them available in the event you have to send an individual email.

7.1.9 Sort It Out; Find It Out

Well let us sort out the details right now. Microsoft Outlook® as well as many email providers allows users to sort their email messages in various arrangements.

Figure 128

- Simply double [click] on the column heading for which you want your email sorted. For example, to see your newest incoming emails, [click] on "Received". If it arranges by first received (hence the oldest emails), then [click] a second time to reverse the order (hence newest received). *(You may have to double click).*
- Want to arrange your email by the sender? Simply [click] the "From" column heading. I have to use this one often because I know I received an email from a certain person, but just cannot remember when.
- Your kids can really benefit from this one once they get into receiving emails on a regular basis.
- I have use the subject also when I send messages to a distribution list and receive multiple replies throughout a couple of days or weeks. [Clicking] the Subject heading helps me to group them all together to see them all at once. After all, each

responding email has replies to the exact same subject line I created.

7.1.10 Screen My Mail

With all of the junk emails out there these days you may want to auto screen some of the important emails. It is just like setting your telephone to ring a special way when certain people call so you will know whether to answer.

Figure 129

Since the book is about helping your family you may want to go as far as to only allow your children's accounts to only receive emails from certain people such as family members and friends. If my children want to start receiving emails from a friend I have to add them to the Safe Senders list.

- [Click] **Actions** on the menu.
- **Select** Junk E-mail.
- **Select** Junk E-mail options.
- Open the **Safe Senders** tab.
- [Click] the **Add** button.
- Type the email address that you consider safe. In this case I have

Figure 130

added the domain names; meaning anyone with those domains (Ex. @bellsouth.net or @pc-mommy.com) is safe. An example would be adding aol.com so that any emails from anyone at AOL such as john124@aol.com and surfchic@aol.com would come through.

- Also check the box at the button that states to "**Include your contacts**".

7.1.11 Away With The Junk

If you do not even want to see the junk then try this one.

- Follow the same steps as setting up the safe list of senders.

Figure 131

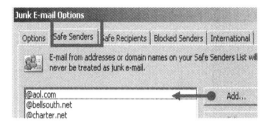

- However, open the **Options** tab.
- <u>Select</u> Safe Lists Only.
- Check the "Permanently delete suspected Junk e-mail" box.

Figure 132

7.1.12 Clean Up My Mailbox Please

- [Click] **Tools**.
- <u>Select</u> Mailbox Cleanup.
- One good thing to do is [click] the Empty button to empty the deleted bin.
- T h

Figure 133

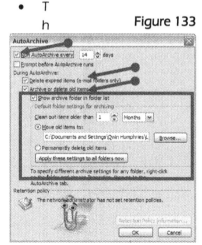

AutoArchive some of the older messages. This will remove them from taking up space in your inbox or wherever to a file folder that can be retrieved later.

- Setup your AutoArchive to run at least every 90 days. I have set mine to every 2 weeks.

- You probably want to be prompted before it runs. I do not want to be bothered though.
- Then setup your default settings as you like.

7.2 Manage It

When I flag a message to delete, I do not want to deal with it anymore. I want it gone the next time I open my Microsoft Outlook®. However, we have to set it up to do this or it will save your deleted messages in a special folder. Also, I like seeing my reading pane on the bottom of my screen so I can sneak a peek at messages when they arrive rather than clicking and opening each one.

Figure 134

- [Click] on **Tools** on the menu and **choose** Options.
- Then [click] on the "**Other**" tab.
- Now check the options you prefer or uncheck the ones you do not.
- Why not check out all of the tabs while you are here?

7.2.1 We Have Rules People

OKAY – you can do a lot of things with this option. However, I will stick with one example where I will create a rule that sends messages from a specific sender (my husband) to my cell phone as a text message. I really do this for my real estate clients so I get their messages immediately. I also set rules that automatically send messages from my students to a separate folder where I keep all of their messages and homework. I also

Figure 135

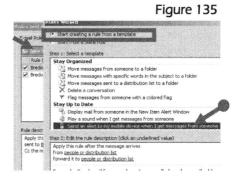

create rules for work that send messages from my boss to a separate folder that is named with her name. I do the same for my coworkers. If anyone has questions about these emails, I can quickly find them because these rules make my system very efficient.

- [Click] **Tools** on the menu and **choose** **Rules and Alerts**.
- Then from the E-mail Rules tab, **choose** "**New Rule**".

Notice that the Rules Wizard guides with steps. So Step 1 (located up top in the window) is to select a template while step 2 (located at the bottom) is to specify to whom and where.

- [Click] "**Send an alert to my mobile device when I get messages from someone**" from the Stay Up to Date section.
- [Click] the **Next** button.

In step 2 you must click the "**From**" link to specify the people or distribution group and also do the same for the "forward" link.

- [Click] "**From people or distribution list**" and double [click] the person or group in your contact list. You can simply type an email address if you would like, but it may be easier to set them up as a contact first. Do this for everyone this rule will apply to and [click] ok.
- Now setup the forwarding details in the same manner, just [click] forward to people or distribution list.
- [Click] in the **To:** field at the bottom of the window and type your cell phone email address. I know mine is my 10 digit phone number followed by *@sprintpcswireless.com*. I actually discovered mine on the Southwest Airlines website under the alert flight details section. You can also add other addresses where the message will be forwarded simultaneously.
- [Click] ok.
- The details shown in the step 2 section should update to the addresses supplied.
- [Click] next until you get to the final rule setup.
- Create a name for this rule such as hubby mail and make sure there is a check in the "Turn the Rule" on box.
- [Click] Finish.
- Simply select a rule and the delete button to remove it or the change button to edit it.

Figure 136

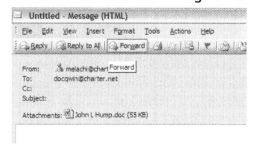

7.2.2 Forward It On

Use the forward button to

www.PC-Mommy.com

Figure 138

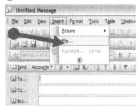

send a message received to another email account. When you [click] **Forward,** insert the email address in the To, CC, or BCC field.

7.2.3 Detach It

One of the best reasons to use email over the phone or via postage is the ease and convenience of sending documents and other files. You will need to teach your children how to detach pictures, documents, or other attachments from a message. Although it is simple to some, it is a process to learn until you get acquainted.

- Open the message that has an attachment. Messages with attachments by default have a gym clip image to the left of the sender's name.

Figure 137

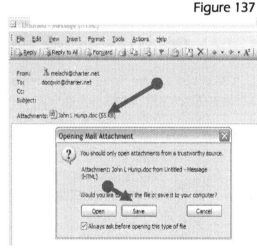

- Look for something that states or indicates the attachment. It usually will say "Attachments" followed by the name of the attached file.
- [Click] the file and either open, save, or download depending on your email provider. I like to save my attachments.

7.2.4 Attach It

- Simply start a new message and [click] the gym clip icon or **Insert** on the menu and **choose** File. (see Figure 138).

105

- Browse and double [click] the file to be attached to the message.
- Complete the email as normal and send when done.

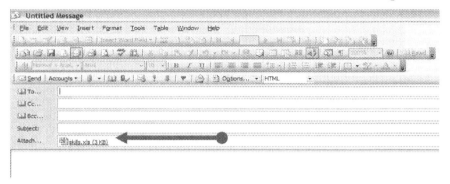

7.2.5 Open Up – This Message Is Important

Figure 140

When you create a message you have the option to flag it with a special flag.

- From your new message, [click] the **Options** button.
- Then set importance to High and Sensitivity to Confidential.
- There are more options you can try as well.

7.2.6 Where, Oh Where, Has My Email Gone

Have you ever wondered . . . "where did that email go?" Now if you are looking for an email from a particular individual you can simply [click] on the **From** heading where your emails will sort into alphabetical order. (Hence [click] a second time if the person or company's name is in the bottom half of the alphabets such as Williams).

106   *www.PC-Mommy.com*

Figure 141

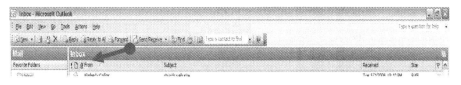

7.2.7 eNews

Save the postage and send those electronic newsletters via email attaching and using the group distribution.

7.2.8 Did You Get It?

You can setup your mail to automatically request a read receipt and/or delivery receipt for confirmation. Just use your **Options** button while creating the email and check the **"Request a read receipt or delivery receipt"** checkboxes. Note: Some systems do not allow read receipts to be sent, however you still can request a delivery receipt.

Figure 143

When the recipient opens the message a read receipt as shown in Figure 143 is sent back to you. If not opened by a certain time you will get the not read receipt as shown in Figure 142.

Figure 142

7.2.9 Cast Your Vote

I like to include people in decisions that affect them. So I use the voting buttons feature to add a vote to the email message. The votes sent back can be tracked automatically in the original email. You do not even have to tally anything.

- When you open a new message window just [click] the **Options** button.
- Then [click] "**Use voting buttons**" in the Voting and Tracking options section. You can change the default options by just typing your choices separated by a semi colon.

Figure 144

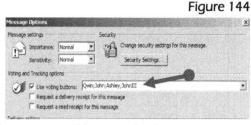

- Then when the email is received by others with Microsoft Outlook®; they would simply [click] on their voting choice (located at the top of the message) and **select** send response.
- The tracking tally and result details automatically update to the original sent message when responders cast their vote. Just open the sent message and [click] the Tracking tab. It is a very nice feature.

Figure 145

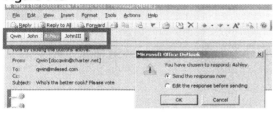

7.2.10 Write It Now, Deliver My Message Later

If you have a message that you would like to create now, but send later then go ahead and create it. However, use your **Options** button to setup a send later. I have tried to remember to send a drafted message and I will forget. Save yourself the hassle of creating a reminder and a draft. Just setup the time and date and contact. Even when you press your send button, the message will await in the outbox folder until it has met the time and date requirements you setup. Warning; it will send on the first initiated send after the date so if you computer is off it will send the next time Microsoft Outlook® is opened.

Figure 146

- [Click] the **Options** button from

your new message window.
- Then check the "**Do not deliver before**" checkbox.
- Setup the earliest date and time you want the message delivered. However, your computer and Internet must be functioning at the time or the message will be delivered as soon as these conditions are met.

7.2.11 Hidden Reminder In The Message

Sometimes we do not want to issue a task or meeting request, but we do want to remind someone about a message we sent. If the Murray's are coming for dinner next Friday then a meeting request probably is not necessary. When you create your email message you have an option to flag that message at the time of composition. Along with the flag you can set an auto reminder for the recipient to help them remember to review or follow up. Otherwise, you may have

Figure 147

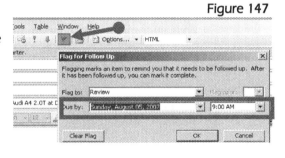

to set yourself a reminder to call and remind them. Do it all at once so when the message is delivered to their inbox along with the reminder.
- Simply [click] the **red flag** icon from within your message window.
- Then setup the "Due by" date and "Time" and the "Type" of flag.
- [Click] ok.

7.3 Contacts

7.3.1 Organize My Peeps

Use the contact view pane on the left side of the screen to switch between different views. I like to see the Detailed Address Cards view so I can see all of the phone numbers. However, you may choose to see a list (phone list), by location, etc.

Figure 148

- Just **select** a view such as "Phone List" or "By Location".
- Try them all just to see. You can also create custom views, which I will not go into details about right now.

7.3.2 Add a Category

Figure 149

Categories can really help when you want to see contacts only related to a certain group. Some of my categories include family, school, work, Real Estate, and clients. When I only want to see family, I can search through 20 numbers instead of 500.

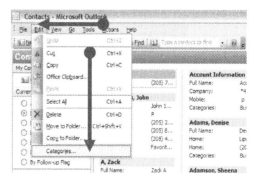

- [Click] **Edit** on the

menu and **choose** Categories.

- Then type the new category and [click] the **Add to list** button.
- When you add the next contact just **choose** that category.

7.3.3 Contact List

Using the phone list view allows you to quickly sort through your contacts. Just [click] on a column header to sort by that column such as "Company".

Figure 150

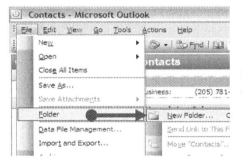

7.3.4 Who's address book is it anyway?

You have the ability to create multiple address books for each computer user of the household.

- Just create a new folder for contact items as shown in Figure 150.

- Remember to **select Contact Items** for the Folder Type. The last time we used Mail and Post Items.
- [Click] Ok.
  The new contact file is created and accessible from the Contact icon/button.
  Remember to select that address book when you are in your Contacts view.

Figure 151

7.3.5 Computer Call Grandma

Figure 152

While in the contacts module, you can **select** a contact and then [click] the **Call** icon (looks like a telephone) or you can **select** the new call option. The **Action** menu also offers a call number option.

Figure 153

You must have a working computer modem to use this function. Since I have a fax machine connected to my phone line I can listen to my current call through the fax speaker. I usually dial out using this "New Call" option and simply pick up the phone if someone answers.

7.3.6 Show Me The Groups

When faced with a large number of emails, contacts, etc. you may choose to group them where you can view a summary style view.

Figure 154

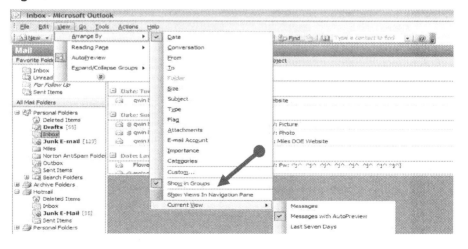

- Simple [click] **View** on the menu and **Arrange By** and then <u>select</u> Groups.
- Expand and collapse the groups accordingly to see full details.

7.4 Tasks

Figure 155

7.4.1 My Own To Do

This is a way to keep up with your To Do list.

- **[Click] Go** on the menu and **<u>choose</u> Tasks** or simply hold Ctrl and press 4.

Figure 156

- The current view options are available on the left side of

the screen. **<u>Select</u>** "**Simple List**". However, you can **select** "**Overdue tasks**" just to see those passed the deadlines or

Figure 157

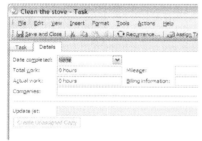

"**Completed tasks**" to see what you have accomplished.

- Now add your 1st task simply by typing the details into the field that says "**Click here to add new task**".
- Type "**Clean the Stove**".
- Press tab and enter the next set of details which most likely will be due date.
- Press enter when done.

Figure 158

7.4.2   My time line

Often times a visual helps us realize things better than words do. This may be the case with your tasks. By using the

timeline view you can see if and how they overlap and adjust your schedule accordingly.

- To view your tasks as a time line just [click] on **Tasks**.
- Then **select** the "**Task Timeline**" view.
- Double [click] the task directly from the timeline to edit.

7.4.3 Your To Do

Just as you can add tasks for yourself, you can create some for others and email it. However, it goes both ways meaning others can create tasks for you too. My son sent me the message to document what he wanted for Christmas one year. You can see in the grey bar that I accepted the task as well as the date and time proposed. See Figure 159. He really did get a mini motorcycle that year too.

Microsoft Outlook® has the capability to monitor tracking as well as send and request status updates. Tell your kids to take a bath and wash their hair. When they are done they would set the task to complete and you will receive an email notification as well as an update in your task list.

Create the task as you would for yourself.

- [Click] the **New** button arrow and **select** New Task request or just right [click] one of yours that you want to designate.
- [Click] the **Assign** button.
- Add the email address in the **To:** field for the person who should be assigned the task.
- Check the "**Keep an updated copy of this task on my task list**"

Figure 159

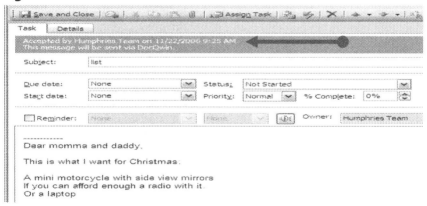

(so you will know what you assigned).

- Check the **send me a status report** when the status is complete. When the assignee checks the task as complete, a "Completed" update status will be sent back to you. Works great at the job also.

7.4.4 Every Week, Once A Month, Reoccurrence

When you setup a task or if you open a new task using the task window, simply [click] the **Recurrence** button to setup a frequency.

- **Select** the pattern in which your task is to reoccur. Whether it is daily for something such as making up your bed, weekly (sweeping the porch), monthly (pay a bill), or yearly (mail Christmas cards) this application can handle it.

- Now indicate how often it is to reoccur in that pattern. If you choose daily then you can select every 2 days, 3 days, everyday, etc.

Figure 160

- For weekly you can choose every Thursday and Friday without including the other days of the week.

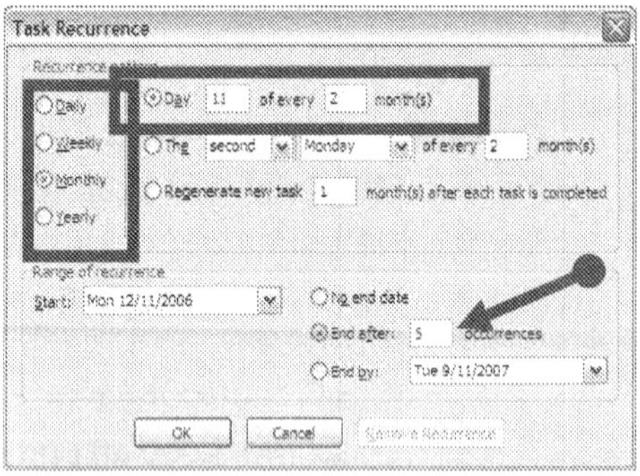

I know at work I have meetings on Fridays so I use this option. For monthly I sometimes setup tasks for every 1st Sunday or last weekday of the month. This helps me on the job also because I have tasks that I have to complete every 1st weekday of the month or a meeting every 3rd Monday of a month. Yearly works the exact same way.

Now there are some tasks I must complete every 3 months so I use the weekly reoccurrence for every Mon, Tues, Wed, Thurs, and Fri. Then I check the regenerate new task every "3" months.

- Finally let us get to the range of the task reoccurrence.

Figure 161

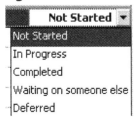

- The start date will default to today's date, but you can change it to the actual date it should start.

7.4.5 Task Manager

The task manager module of Microsoft Outlook® allows you to setup your to do list electronically. This is a nice feature because you can setup reminders to alert you when a task should be almost done, set a percentage to track how much you have done, and so much more. However, when you set the date and times, the tasks do not appear on your calendar cluttering your space. Instead they appear in the task manager.

- You can either [click] on the **Tasks** button/icon to see a full view or view a smaller list in your calendar view as a task pad. Simply switch the views to manage your task in different ways. Use the **Next Seven Days** view to see upcoming tasks.
- <u>Select</u> By **Person Responsible** to sort through the assigned tasks. Or simply double [click] a column header to sort ascending or descending by that column such as **Due Date** or **Requested by**. The **owner** is the person assigned to complete the task. Try them out and discover what works for you and your family and for you at work.

7.4.6 How Far Have You Gotten?

An assignee may simply right [click] a task and <u>select</u> a status update. As long as you are tracking a percentage, it is as easy as that.

7.5 *Calendar*

7.5.1 Weekly Schedule

Your calendar can be viewed in different ways. While the calendar is
open, (to open just [click] your calendar button), simply [click] the 1 day, 5 work week, 7 week, or 31 month button. Your appointments show as blocks. Double [click] on a text block to open the

Figure 162

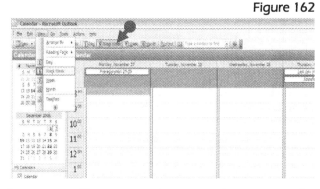

appointment. You can always press Alt + any number to see that amount of days. For example, Alt + 3 will show 3 days.

7.5.2 Color My Appointments

- Right [click] on a date in your calendar to open your shortcut menu.

Figure 163

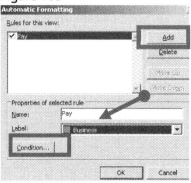

- Click **Automatic Format**.
- Click the **Add** button.
- Type a name to identify this coloring in the name field so you can refer back to it later.
- **Choose** a label color, which will be applied to every block that you meet the conditions you are about to setup.
- [Click] the **Condition** button.

- A new window opens. Type a word to be searched for in every appointment. When found, Outlook will change the color of the block to the color you chose. I am going to type the word "Pay".

- Then make sure the "In:" field is set to subject field only if you plan to always place "Pay" in the subject field. Change if necessary.

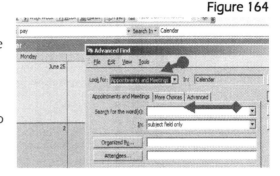

Figure 164

- I am not going to use an "Organized by", but you can if you want
- You can explore the other tabs which help you further narrow your criteria.
- [Click] ok.

7.5.3 Print My Schedule

Anytime you want to print a copy of your calendar just open your calendar window so you can see it.
- Click **File** on the menu and <u>select</u> Print.
- In the Print window <u>choose</u> the **Print style**. For instance <u>choose</u> **Monthly** to print the entire month.
- Then in the **Print date range** <u>select</u> the dates to be included in the calendar. Just [click] the arrow next to the start date field to open a calendar selector.
- Click **Preview** to see what your print job will look like.

Figure 165

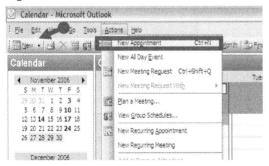

- Then [click] **Print** to actually print your calendar.

7.5.4 Set An Appointment

This is almost like your

119

task request.

- However, you can simply double [click] the date on the calendar or [click] the **New** button or arrow.
- Then enter the information for the appointment such as date, time, subject, etc.
- [Click] **Save and Close** when you are done setting up.

Figure 166

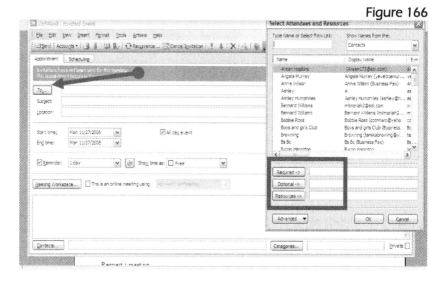

7.5.5 Request a Meeting

Let us try to get a family meeting together where everyone can give input on their schedules.

- Press **Ctrl + Shift + Q** or go to **New** and <u>select</u> **New Meeting**

Figure 167

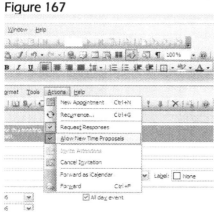

Request.

- Now [click] the **To**: button to open your "**Select Attendees and Resources**" window.
- <u>Select</u> the name of the first invitee and then [click] the required button if they are required to come or

otherwise the optional button.

- You can also just type an email address in the appropriate field ("Required" or "Optional").
- To add someone new to your contacts while you are in the "**Select Attendees**" window just [click] the **Advanced** button and follow the directions.
- Repeat until all the names are added.
- To set or disable counter proposals [click] the **Actions** button.
- [Click] the **Allow New Time Proposals** item.

7.5.6   Find My Appointment

On the same toolbar with the calendar style buttons (1 day, 31 month, etc.) there is also a find button that can search for words.

- Click the **Find** button.
- Type the text to search for and [click] **Find**.
- To perform and advanced search [click] the **Options** button located at the top right and <u>select</u> **Advanced Find**.
- Now you may enter an organizer to search for and other details as warranted.

7 . 6 *Journal*

Easily document your day's events.

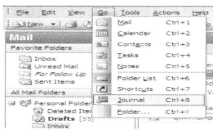

Figure 168

7.6.1 My Diary

I can remember having to keep a journey in school and how hard it was to think of things to write in the beginning. However, it was pretty neat after a while. It is a great thinking exercise and can even help you get things off of your chest. Why not have the family spend 10 minutes a day writing in their journals? Using the Journal is a breeze.

- Just [click] on the **Journal** button or icon.
- **Choose** the entry type. Just use Document to start.
- [Click] the **Start Timer** button and simply start typing.
- The timer tracks your time for you so just keep going until you reach your desired time. I may go for 5 or 10 minutes.
- [Click] the **Pause Timer** button when you are interrupted.
- Remember to set a category (bottom right corner button) if you would like to organize your journal into categories.

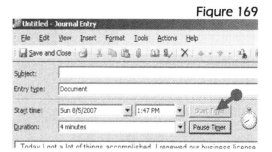

Figure 169

7.7 *Notes*

7.7.1 Sticky Notes

I remember when I first saw the Sticky Post It Notes. They can be very handy except maybe when you have too many or they stop sticking. However, I still use them all of the time now. Using the Notes module allows us to create some small notes or memos that you can easily refer back to.

Figure 170

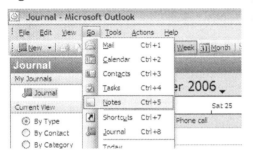

- [Click] **Go** on the Menu and **select Notes**. Notice the shortcut is **Ctrl key + 5**.
- Now [click] the **New** button.
- A small yellow square resembling a sticky note appears. Type your info and [click] the "**X**" in the upper right corner of the note to save it.
- If you want to see the note in the full screen, simply double [click] the top bar of the note.

Figure 171

- Double [click] to restore the smaller view.

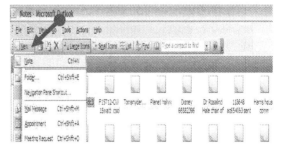

I like to keep important numbers and quick notes. I have my Southwest Rewards Member number and things like that in my notes.

7.7.2 Colorful Notes

All of your notes do not have to be yellow. You many want some green, pink, or blue. I do not color code mine because I sync them to my cell phone to have my information accessible wherever I have my phone. You or your family may want may want try this color coding method to see how it works. What if your hubby asks for the Tax ID number to the day care? No problem – it is in a note. What time do to the kids take lunch (something I just cannot seem to remember)? Check the sticky. Okay, it is not really "stickable", but it is handy. Let us see what we can do with the notes. Make sure you have a note created.

Figure 172

- Right [click] the Note.
- [Click] color to change the color.
- [Click] **Forward** to send the note via email to someone else. There is no sense in having everyone create the same identical note when you can simply pass it on.

7.7.3   Save Notes As A Document

Open the Note you want to save as a text document outside of the Microsoft Outlook® application.

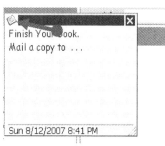

Figure 173

- [Click] the **Notes Options** icon in the top left corner of the note.
- [Click] **Save As.**
- Save with the name and in the location of your choice.

7.8 Others

7.8.1 AutoCorrect Text

This feature can come in very handy for the common text you include in your documents. It helps you create short text that will automatically convert to the true longer text when inserted. An example would be setting your initials "QJH" to automatically convert to Qwin J. Humphries, M.Ed. That saves me from typing my full name all of the time. Also it can be great for words you know you commonly misspell. Just setup the misspelled word to automatically correct to the correctly spelled word. How about we see it in action? Remember you can set this up in Microsoft Word® as well.

- [Click] **Tools** on the menu and **select Options.**
- [Click] the **Spelling** tab.
- Check the **Use AutoCorrect when Word isn't the editor** checkbox.
- [Click] the **AutoCorrect Options** button.
- In the **Replace** field, type the text that will be corrected and replaced. "QH"
- In the **With** field, type the correct text that will replace the short text. "Qwin Humphries"
- [Click] the **Add** button.
- [Click] Ok.
- You can replace or delete any of your AutoCorrect words at anytime by **selecting** the word and [clicking] **Replace** or **Delete**.

7.8.2 Right Click And Drag

Drag your files to Microsoft Outlook® directly from a folder on your computer. Attach one or several files to a message, link files to a journal, or merely save a file in your inbox with just a drag and drop. This is a good way to place files in a central location and setup reminders for you and your family to review them. It also works great to help keep your work team on target with projects. Let us break these down.

Drag and attach:

- Open the folder where the file resides and make sure you can still see your inbox. If your folder is not in view, simply [click] the **Restore down** button located at the top right of the screen. See Figure 174.

Figure 174

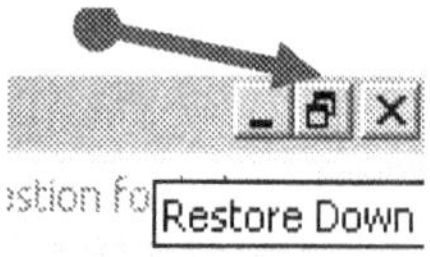

- Resize the window by dragging one of the corner handles inward.
- Now open the folder that contains your picture. In my case I will open my "**My Pictures**" folder.
- Hold down the Ctrl key and <u>select</u> all the pictures you want to include.
- Right [click] the selection and drag them directly into Microsoft Outlook® and onto the button or icon. I am dragging three pictures onto the Mail icon so I can attach them to a message. Note: If you [click] and drag rather than right [click] and drag you will send a shortcut to the file rather than the actual file. Files on your computer most likely will not be accessible to others so use the right [click].
- You will be prompted with some options, <u>choose</u> **Send with attachment**.
- Now create your email message and notice the files are attached to the message. To add more files to the message simply <u>select</u> them in the folder and drag and drop them to the attachment field. Alternatively, you can use the traditional **Insert** menu and <u>choose</u> **File**.

Drag a shortcut

- Let us send a shortcut to a document in my "**My Documents**" folder to the calendar.
- [Click] the document and drag it to the calendar button or icon. By [clicking] we automatically send a shortcut rather than attachment.
- A new appointment window opens with the subject defaulted to the file name. An icon is located in the Content section.
- Double [click] the file shortcut icon to open. It will open as long as the file exists in the same location with the same name.

126   *www.PC-Mommy.com*

Now let us add a file to your Inbox without attaching.

- **<u>Select</u>** a file and then right [click] and drag it to your Inbox folder. You may choose another folder if you would like.
- **<u>Choose</u> Copy**.

There you go. The file is listed along with your incoming messages. You may choose to forward it or flag it and even set a reminder flag. I use this one on the job for travel. If I leave important files at work, which I do, I can simply open my email via the web and there are those documents.

8 In Conclusion

I thank you for taking interest in my book. Hopefully if you utilize some of my ideas at home you will become more proficient over time. For me, that meant becoming more efficient and effective at work. That equated to several promotions and a successful career change. These are just ideas that I have been trying or planning for a couple of years.

If you have some interesting ideas then post them on my website: www.PC-Mommy.com. Refer this book to a mother, daughter, sister, or significant other. Let us help each other become the greatest technology family experts. Please visit the website to find out more information about learning, teaching, speaking, or consulting opportunities.

Good luck to you and your family.

[Click], [click]! - Qwin

Appendix: My Favorite Keyboard Shortcuts

I love the mouse because I started using computers when there was just a keyboard, but I can sometimes move around much quicker using some quick keyboard strokes.

My favorites keyboard shortcuts are:

Ctrl + Z	Undo
F7	Spell-check
Shift + F7	Thesaurus
Ctrl + A	Select All
Ctrl + N	New
Ctrl + O	Open
Ctrl + P	Print
Ctrl + H	Find and Replace
Ctrl + Home	Return to the Top Document
Ctrl + End	Go to the End of the Document
Ctrl +	Delete Word
Ctrl + C	Copy
Ctrl + V	Paste
Ctrl + CC	Open Clipboard

www.ingramcontent.com/pod-product-compliance
Lightning Source LLC
Chambersburg PA
CBHW051246050326
40689CB00007B/1082